HENRY JAMES

HARRY T. MOORE

HENRY JAMES

THAMES AND HUDSON

Frontispiece: Henry James during his
American tour in 1905.

© 1974 Thames and Hudson Ltd,
London

First published in paperback in the
United States of America in 1999 by
Thames and Hudson Inc., 500 Fifth
Avenue, New York, New York 10110

Library of Congress Catalog Card
Number 98-61522
ISBN 0-500-26032-X

Printed and bound in Spain

THE GRANDFATHER OF HENRY JAMES was a Protestant Irishman from County Cavan who in 1789 emigrated to America, as one of his descendants noted, 'with a little money, a Latin grammar (which still exists), and a great desire to visit one of the Revolutionary battlefields'. He was eighteen years old.

By 1793 this William James (1771–1832) had settled in Albany, in upstate New York, soon to become the state capital. It was a neat Dutch town, with corbie-gabled houses and streets of cobble-stone, at that period crowded with ox-carts and with men pointing towards the western lands. The lively young immigrant prospered from the first. Beginning as a clerk, he soon became an independent merchant and the owner of extensive real estate. He was prominent enough in 1823 to be the official orator at the opening of the Erie Canal, which linked Albany to the Great Lakes. When he died nine years later he left three million dollars, the largest fortune in New York State after that of John Jacob Astor.

His career was a typical American success-story, containing the familiar elements of frontier adventure and capitalist enterprise. But his descendants cared little for commerce, expecially in the branch of the family which included his novelist-grandson, who once observed, 'The rupture with my grandfather's tradition and attitude was complete; we were never in a single case, I think, for two generations, guilty of a stroke of business.'

Albany, New York, as it looked when the grandfather of Henry James was one of its most prominent and successful citizens. The corbie-gabled house at right was the former home of the early Dutch governors.

A view of the Erie Canal where it joined the Hudson River at Albany, creating a water link between the Eastern seaboard and the Great Lakes.

Catherine Barber James, about 1855.

Certainly Henry James the elder (1811–82) – the second surviving son of his father's third marriage, to Catherine Barber, the Scottish-Irish daughter of a judge – discovered early that he had no interest in business. Nor did he care for the rigidly applied Calvinist faith of his father, a faith which, by regulating his children's inheritance, sought to control them even from the grave. The children took the will to court and succeeded in having it broken. The elder Henry James was awarded a settlement that left him 'leisured for life'.

One of the most important events of his youth occurred when he was thirteen years old. In helping to put out a fire in a stable, he was burned so severely in one leg that it had to be amputated above the knee, and he was confined to bed for two years. The accident did little to reduce his liveliness, which later manifested itself in conviviality at college and in energetic activities throughout his life: rearing a family, travelling extensively, and writing copiously.

He became a religious philosopher. He was trained in theological dialectic, first at Union College in Schenectady, New York, and then at the seminary at Princeton, New Jersey. But he discovered that orthodox creeds produced a ritual of outward behaviour rather than a worship of the spirit. He later found satisfaction in the theological doctrines of Emanuel Swedenborg.

In 1840 the elder Henry James married Mary Robertson Walsh, sister of a Princeton friend. She was Scottish-Irish, like his mother, and she lived in New York City. Her mother was the widow of a wealthy cotton merchant.

The couple's first child was William (1842–1910), the philosopher and psychologist. Henry (1843–1916) was next, followed by Garth

Wilkinson ('Wilky' 1845–83), Robertson (1846–1910), and Alice (1848–92). Throughout childhood they all travelled extensively, often in the Europe whose glamour attracted the second son so much that at last he settled there.

The continual restless moves of the family were the result of the elder Henry James's desire to provide the best possible education for his children. Once when he was taking them abroad he wrote to his friend Ralph Waldo Emerson to explain that he was uprooting them so that they might 'absorb French and German and get a better sensuous education than they are likely to get here'.

The mother was a stabilizing element. The younger Henry James wrote at the time of her death in 1882 that she had been 'the sweetest, gentlest, most natural embodiment of maternity – and our protecting spirit, our household genius'.

The New York in which Henry James was born on 15 April 1843 was a small city nestling at the lower end of Manhattan Island. The environs of Washington Square were then on the way to becoming fashionable; the house of James's birth, 21 Washington Place, is now gone, replaced by a New York University building. The house itself, of the rose-coloured brick that characterized the area, was probably similar to the one described as Dr Sloper's in Henry James's short novel *Washington Square*, a building which 'exactly resembled' those around it, 'a handsome, modern, wide-fronted house, with a big balcony before the drawing-room windows, and a flight of white marble steps ascending to a portal which was also faced with white marble'.

William James the Elder, of Albany, the enterprising businessman who bequeathed to his numerous children a legacy of Calvinist fear and prohibitions.

(*Overleaf*) New York in 1867. Within a dozen years of the James family's departure, the city had been transformed from 'the small warm dusty homogeneous . . . world' that Henry always remembered.

The National Guard on parade in Washington Square, near the house where Henry James was born.

Young Henry was soon taken away from Washington Place, for when he was only six months old his father transported the little family to Europe for two years, during which time they stayed in both England and France. In England, the father underwent a nervous crisis, beginning in May 1844 with a terrible vision, a feeling that a demon of some kind had appeared to him. He remained for more than two years in a state of intermittent terrors, which doctors could not alleviate. A Mrs Chichester whom he met at a watering-place advised that he try Swedenborg, with whose work he was unfamiliar.

Mrs Chichester suggested that James was undergoing what Swedenborg termed a 'vastation', that is, one stage in the human regenerative process, an awakening by means of which he could be reborn, achieve independence and confront his God without fear. James hurried to obtain the works of the Swedish scientist and prophet, and as he read them he felt the oppressive terrors leave him. He became a lifelong devotee of Swedenborg's writings, though he adapted them to his own temperament and needs.

On little Henry's first trip abroad he also experienced a revelation of sorts. He was then two years old. It was not of a shattering nature, like his father's, but it was significant. He coined his first memory, and it was appropriate that this should be a European memory. In his auto-biographical volume *A Small Boy and Others* (1913), James recalled:

I had been there [in Europe] for a short time in the second year of my life, and I was to communicate to my parents later on that as a baby in long clothes, seated opposite to them in a carriage and on the lap of another person, I had been impressed with the view, framed by the clear window of the vehicle as we passed, of a great stately square surrounded with high-roofed houses and having in its centre a tall and glorious column. I had naturally caused them to marvel but I had also, under cross-questioning, forced them to compare notes, as it were, and reconstitute the miracle. They knew what my observation of monumental squares had been – and alas hadn't; neither New York nor Albany could have offered me the splendid perspective, and, for that matter, neither could London, which moreover I had known at a younger age still. Conveyed along the rue St Honoré while I waggled my small feet, as I definitely remember doing, under my flowing robe, I had crossed the rue de Castiglione and taken in, for all my time, the admirable aspect of the Place and the Colonne Vendôme.

We may note that in writing this passage when he was about seventy, Henry James couldn't keep out a sigh because, by the age of five, his experience of interesting cities had not been greater than it was.

His autobiographical volume also mentioned Albany, where he had been taken soon after the family's return from Europe, an Albany of 'swarming cousinship' and 'of the Dutch houses and the steep streets and the recurrent family names – Townsends, Clintons, Van Rensselaers, Pruyns', a town whose 'sweet taste . . . probably lurked more in its being our admired antithesis to New York; it was holiday, whereas New York was home'.

He went to his first schools in Albany and in New York City, remembering long afterwards his introduction to kindergarten at Albany when he was three: his brother William, sixteen months older, looked on in wonder as Henry howled and kicked so vehemently in the doorway that the beginning of his education had to be post-poned.

The ten years which the James family spent in America between their return to the United States in 1845 and their next trip to Europe in 1855 was the longest consecutive residence in his native land that Henry James the younger was ever to know. After trying Albany in 1845–47, his father finally settled the family in a large old house at 58 West Fourteenth Street, in the midst of what his novelist-son would recall as 'the small warm dusty homogeneous New York world of the mid-century'.

He later wrote that 'Broadway was the feature and the artery, the joy and the adventure of one's childhood, and it stretched, and pro-digiously, from Union Square to Barnum's Great American Museum by the City Hall.' After he and William had attended school at Mrs

Henry James's earliest memory was 'of a great stately square surrounded with high-roofed houses and having in its centre a tall and glorious column' – the Colonne Vendôme in Paris.

Broadway, with Barnum's Great
American Museum, about 1850.

Lavinia D. Wright's on East Twenty-first Street, they would return
home by way of Fourth Avenue, where the Hudson River Railroad
was then being built, 'or was being made to traverse the upper reaches
of the city, through that part of which raged, to my young sense, a riot
of explosion and a great shouting and waving of red flags when the
groundpowder introduced into the rocky soil was about to take
effect'. The brothers and some of their schoolmates felt it was a point
of honour 'nobly to defy the danger' of the explosions which hurled
rocks into the air. That the young Henry James didn't always take the
risk, he inferred

from the memory of other perambulations of the period – as to which I am divided
between their still present freshness and my sense of perhaps making too much of
these tiny particles of history. My stronger rule, however, I confess, and the one by
which I must here consistently be guided, is that, from the moment it is a question of

A typical scene of construction in Manhattan as the city spread north-wards with 'a riot of explosion and a great shouting'.

projecting a picture, no particle that counts for memory or is appreciable to the spirit, *can* be too tiny, and that experience, in the name of which one speaks, is all compact of them and shining with them. . . .

– a passage in which James gives away one of the secrets of his own vision as a writer, his urge to be as conclusive as possible.

The boy met several notable men at this time. Emerson was an occasional visitor, and the James children called the guest-room 'Mr Emerson's room'. There were also Washington Irving and General Winfield Scott. And callers came from abroad, one of them William Makepeace Thackeray, who said, 'Come here, little boy, and show me your extraordinary jacket!'

Smoky rooms with black stoves characterized the schools the boys went to, usually for only a brief period until their dissatisfied father would withdraw them to try another. He didn't want them to become

Brady's Daguerreotype Gallery on Broadway where the photograph on page 15 was taken.

prigs, and he despised training that stressed the literal and the pedantic.

In 1854 the two Henry Jameses were put on to a daguerreotype by Matthew Brady, later to become the classic photographer of the American Civil War, but already famous, with a studio on Broadway. The father with his fringe of whiskers looks like a stage Irishman in this picture, which has little in common with Frank Duveneck's portrait of the long-bearded man of a quarter-century later (whom Emerson's son thought of as looking like Socrates). A solemn little boy with large brown eyes, young Henry stands beside his father, wearing the jacket that had caught the eye of Thackeray.

'I repaired with my father on an August day to the great Broadway establishment of Mr Brady, supreme in that then beautiful art. . . . I remember the "exposure" as on this occasion interminably long, yet with the result of a facial anguish far less harshly reproduced than my suffered snapshots of a later age.' (*A Small Boy and Others*)

The shyness so evident in the picture revealed itself further in his inability to acquire friends of his own age. He found 'all boys . . . difficult to play with'. His elder brother William once boasted to him, '*I* play with boys who curse and swear.' Henry didn't. And although he became in time an intimate and popular member of European literary and social circles, he had in childhood developed the necessary inwardness of the artist, which remained with him despite all his later conviviality.

Reading became a habit. One of his boyhood favourites was Dickens, whom the young admirer had a chance to see dramatized

One item from Barnum's Gallery of Wonders.

when several of the novels were turned into plays in New York. On the stage he also saw some Shakespeare, but much more of nine-teenth-century melodrama.

Much later, remembering these New York years, James wrote:

I turn round again to where I last left myself gaping at the old ricketty bill-board in Fifth Avenue; and am almost as sharply aware as ever of the main source of its spell, the fact that it most often blazed with the rich appeal of Mr Barnum, whose 'lecture room', attached to the Great American Museum, overflowed into posters of all the theatrical bravery disavowed by its title. It was my rueful theory of those days . . . that on all the holidays on which we weren't dragged to the dentist's we attended as a matter of course at Barnum's. . . . I have . . . the whole undimmed sense of the . . . weary waiting, in the dusty halls of humbug, amid bottled mermaids, 'bearded ladies' and chill dioramas, for the lecture-room, the true centre of the seat of joy, to open: vivid in especial to me is my almost sick wondering of whether I mightn't be rapt away before it did open. The impression appears to have been mixed; the drinking deep and the holding out, holding out in particular against the failure of food and of stage-fares, provision for transport to and fro, being questions equally intense: the appeal of the lecture-room, in its essence a heavy extra, so exhausted our resources that even the sustaining doughnut of the refreshment counter would mock our desire and the long homeward crawl, the length of Broadway and further, seem to defy repetition. Those desperate days, none the less, affect me now as having flushed with the very complexion of romance; their aches and inanitions were part of the adventure; the homeward straggle, interminable as it appeared, flowered at moments into rapt contemplations – that for instance of the painted portrait, large as life, of the celebrity of the hour, then 'dancing' at the Broadway Theatre, Lola Montes, Countess of Lansfeldt, of a dazzling and unreal beauty and in a riding-habit lavishly open at the throat.

In 1855, when the family went abroad again, the twelve-year-old Henry was eagerly ready for the trip. His reading (among other things, of *Punch*, which brought him close to British life and humour, particularly in the drawings of John Leech), his attendance at operas and concerts where European music was played, his receptivity to both painting and sculpture, his father's brilliant visitors from abroad – all these quickened the boy's desire to cross the ocean again and to revisit the Paris of his earliest memory.

The boy's thoughts of Europe were refreshed on that trip, and he intensely felt the magnetism of foreign lands. His father permitted the family to remain only a few days in London, where young Henry, who

Cartoons such as this by John Leech helped to form young Henry's early impressions of British life and humour.

had come down with malarial chills and fever, spent most of his time in bed. The boy's appreciation of Paris was marked by 'the intensity of a fond apprehension' of the place,

from the balcony of an hotel that hung, through the soft summer night, over the rue de la Paix. I hung with the balcony, and doubtless with my brothers and my sister, though I recover what I felt as so much relation and response to the larger, the largest appeal only, that of the whole perfect Parisianism I seemed to myself always to have possessed mentally – even if I had but just turned twelve! – and that now filled out its frame or case for me from every lighted window, up and down, as if each of these had been, for strength of sense, a word in some immortal quotation, the very breath of civilized lips.

His father's goal was Geneva, and to reach it from Paris in those days, people went by rail as far as Lyons, and then took a coach that rolled and bumped them to their destination. The sick boy travelled with a special plank-and-mattress bed in which he could lie still as he looked at the whirling landscapes. He enjoyed the trip.

One day the father ordered a halt at a Jura village where young Henry looked up to see a ruined castle far above. It was his first vision of such a place. He saw, at the bottom of the hill below the castle, a peasant woman in wooden shoes, white shirt and red petticoat.

Supremely, in that ecstatic vision, was 'Europe', sublime synthesis, expressed and guaranteed to me – as if by a mystic gage, which spread all through the summer air, that I should now, only now, never lose it, hold the whole consistency of it: up to that time it might have been but mockingly whisked before me. Europe mightn't have been flattered, it was true, in my finding her thus most signified and summarized in a sordid old woman scraping a mean living and an uninhabitable tower abandoned to the owls. That was but the momentary measure of a small sick boy, however, and the virtue of the impression was proportioned to my capacity. It made a bridge over more things than I then knew.

The family didn't stay long amid 'the fine old houses of the Cité' and 'the sturdily seated lakeside villas' of Geneva; the father at first praised the schools there, but after two months they disappointed him, so the Jameses all went back to Paris for another brief stay, and then on to London, where they took a house in Berkeley Square, later moving on to one in St John's Wood, from whose windows the boys could see men and women practising archery. Writing in 1913, Henry James said of 1855–56 London that

It was extraordinarily the picture and the scene of Dickens, now so changed and superseded; it offered to my presumptuous vision still more the reflection of Thackeray . . . so that as I trod the vast length of Baker Street, the Thackerayan vista of other days, I throbbed with the pride of a vastly enlarged acquaintance.

The children had a succession of tutors, and they visited not only Madame Tussaud's exhibition of wax figures, but also various theatres and art museums, and such landmarks as the Tower of

London, Westminster Abbey, and St Paul's, as well as the National Gallery.

In the summer of 1856, the family once more moved to Paris, where again the children had tutors and visited the notable places. Paris was not so beautiful then as it was to become after being Haussmannized with the grand boulevards: 'Its connections with the past, however, still hung thickly on; its majesties and symmetries, comparatively vague and general, were subject to the happy accident, the charming lapse and the odd extrusion, a bonhomie of chance composition and colour now quite purged away.' James had a lifelong and rather secret admiration of Napoleon I, whose presence he felt during his boyhood days in the Paris of the Second Empire. The glory and power of the Napoleonic past had come to vivid life for James upon his first visit to the magnificent Galerie d'Apollon in the Louvre, which had so impressed him that it figured much later as the scene of a dream he always remembered as 'the most appalling yet most admirable nightmare of my life'.

The main street of Boulogne-sur-mer in the 1850s.

In the middle 1850s the James family stayed twice in the grey seaport-town of Boulogne-sur-mer, with another interval in Paris. From Boulogne in October 1857, the elder James said in a letter, 'Harry is not so fond of study, properly so called, as of reading. He is a devourer of libraries, and an immense writer of novels and dramas.' When Henry was attending the Collège Impérial at Boulogne, he became a friend of one of his fellow students, the future actor Constant Coquelin, the first to play Cyrano de Bergerac in the drama which Edmond Rostand wrote for him near the end of the century; in Boulogne, the James boys rather envied Coquelin because his father operated the finest pastry shop in town, always full of delectable cakes. In later years James wrote of 'the dreary months' at Boulogne, a dreariness no doubt increased by his having come down with typhus, the gravest illness of his life until the last and fatal one.

Boulogne eventually bored his parents, and the father, again looking for an excuse to move, announced that American schools were really better than European. Hence in 1858 the family returned to the United States, settling at Newport, Rhode Island, where the elder James had friends. This was not the fashionable Newport of later years, but a small and 'shabby' place, full of eighteenth-century houses, grass coming up between the cobble-stones and promontories stretching out to the sea. William and Henry soon acquired friends of their own, Henry at fifteen having lost some of his shyness. These friends included the artist John La Farge, somewhat older than the James boys, and Thomas Sergeant ('Sargy') Perry, later a critic and editor.

In 1859 the elder James quite typically declared that he felt discouraged about American education and would once more take his children to Europe. In a letter to a friend, he said,

(*Below left*) The painter John La Farge, seven years older than Henry James, became one of his closest friends at Newport, encouraging his literary interests and introducing him to the works of Balzac and Mérimée.

(*Below right*) Henry James at Geneva, aged sixteen.

I have but one *fixed mind* about anything; which is, that whether we stay here or go abroad, and whatever befalls my dear boys in this world, they and you and I are all alike, and after all, absolute creatures of God, vivified every moment by Him, cared for every moment by Him, guided every moment by an infallible wisdom and an irreproachable tenderness, and that we have none of us therefore the slightest right to indulge any anxiety or listen in any conceivable circumstances to the lightest whisper of perturbation.

On that European trip, the Jameses went to Germany and Switzerland, staying once more at Geneva, 'on the edge of the rushing Rhône'. There, William attended the Academy which was to become the university, Wilky and Robertson went to a near-by boarding-school, and little Alice remained with her parents. Henry found himself at a local technical school, not as preparation for a career, but apparently because his father wanted him to learn science. As young Henry wrote to Sargy Perry, 'The school is intended for preparing such boys as wish to be engineers, architects, machinists, "and the like" for higher schools, and I am the only one who is not destined for either of the useful arts or sciences, although I am, I hope, for the art of being useful in some way.' After the spring vacation, his father let him drop out of all except the language courses. He attended lecture sessions at William's school, and even went with his brother to the laboratory where corpses were dissected, but the stench overwhelmed him, greatly to William's amusement.

The father soon made another shift: William, Henry and Wilky were to undertake the burden of German education in Beethoven's native town, Bonn. William and Henry, accompanied by a guide

The Hôtel de l'Ecu in Geneva, where Henry lived with his parents in 1859–60 while attending a local technical school.

with a mule, walked along the edges of the Alps as far as Interlaken. While staying overnight at the Hospice of St Bernard, they again encountered corpses, this time of travellers who had frozen to death attempting to cross the mountains. They were kept in a special mortuary. Henry described the scene in a letter to Sargy Perry: 'As they cannot be buried they are stood around the walls in their shrouds and a grim and ghastly sight it is. They fall into all sorts of hideous positions, with such fiendish grins on their faces! Faugh!'

At Interlaken Henry and William joined their parents and Wilky and Alice, and they all proceeded into Germany. At Bonn, William was lodged with one family, Henry and Wilky with another, under the care of 'a pair of kindly pedagogues'. Henry always remembered the Rhenish wine, served in 'long-necked bottles, with rather chalky cakes, in that forward section of our general eating-and-living room' with its 'unbroken space . . . lighted at either end, from street and court, and its various effects of tempered shade, or, frankly speaking, of rather greasy gloom'.

The Hospice of St Bernard. 'The sky is of a liquid twinkling sort of blue, and the gigantic grey and white rocks rise up against it so sharply-cut and so barren . . .'. (*Letters*)

(*Above left*) William James at twenty-five.

(*Above right*) Minny Temple, who was later to serve James as the model for several of his fictional heroines. Her hair had been cropped short because of illness.

The James boys in the daytime wandered along the Rhine and even went to the place Byron had called 'the castled crag of Drachenfels'. Before long, William told his father that he wished to study painting seriously and that he wanted to be a student of William Morris Hunt's in Newport. In September 1860 the Jameses sailed for America again, and once more went to the Rhode Island seaside town.

Hunt, who had studied painting in Paris, was the American deputy of the Barbizon school of French artists, which included Corot, Millet and Théodore Rousseau. William James had some talent as a painter, Henry very little. But the younger brother, from his art work with Hunt and his conversations with La Farge, developed an intimacy with studio life which was to serve him well in many of his stories. Sargy Perry remembered that Henry, in an earnest attempt to become a writer, at this time also translated plays by Alfred de Musset and tales of Prosper Mérimée, which no periodical published.

At Newport James encountered his cousin Mary ('Minny') Temple, a girl who liked both merry parties and serious conversations. As James later said, 'She was the heroine of our common scene.' Regrettably, her only surviving photograph shows her with her hair cropped because of illness, and gives but little hint of the charm which so many young men found in her.

The Civil War burst over the land in the spring of 1861, and many young men of New England volunteered at once. William and Henry James hung back; the former, who had decided he wasn't a painter went to a scientific school at Harvard, while Henry remained at home. They never did go to war, though their younger brothers eventually enlisted and distinguished themselves in battle. Robertson passed through the conflict unscathed, but Wilky was wounded in 1863.

In October 1861, the younger Henry James suffered what he later termed a 'horrid even if obscure hurt'. One day a fire raged in New-port, burning a cluster of stables and threatening near-by residences. Young Henry was among others trying to induce 'a rural, a rusty, a quasi-extemporized old engine to work' so that 'a saving stream would flow'. While 'jammed into the acute angle between two fences', he sustained an injury which, as he recognized from the first, was to be long lasting in its effects. Throughout his life he occasionally referred to this injury, and several commentators have imagined that James was castrated. (Some psychoanalysts find in the 'hurt' a *mimesis* or compulsive, unconscious, imitation of his father who in his own youth had been severely injured in putting out a fire.) Leon Edel, who has mustered all the evidence connected with the 'horrid even if obscure hurt', finds that it points clearly to a back injury – a slipped disc, a sacroiliac or muscular strain – obscure but clearly painful. Apparently because of his 'obscure hurt' James didn't follow his younger brothers and various friends into the Union Army.

(*Below left*) The outbreak of the American Civil War in April 1861 provoked the crisis of a nation – and a generation. Although he did not join the fighting, Henry James never forgot the 'tang in the atmosphere' and the 'flagrant difference . . . in the look of everything' during the war years. (*Notes of a Son and Brother*)

(*Below right*) A sketch by William James of his brother Wilky in bed, convalescing from his Civil War wounds.

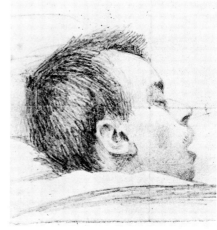

The James family home in Newport,
Rhode Island, 1860–62.

The dining-room in Hyanuary,
Brazil, used by members of the
Louis Agassiz zoölogical expedition.

Like William, Henry gave up his work with Hunt. William had weak eyes and, since the return to Newport, had developed a nervous malady which affected his digestion. After three years at the scientific school at Harvard, he enrolled as a medical student of the college in 1864, and in the following year joined Louis Agassiz's zoölogical expedition to Brazil. There he had a violent attack of what was probably smallpox. In 1867 he went to Germany, attending the University of Berlin and sometimes going to the resort of Bad Teplitz.

In 1862 Henry had undertaken the study of law at Harvard, in those days when Cambridge was almost completely rural. But the law didn't grip him, and when he left Harvard at the end of the school year he was beginning to realize that he would become a full-time writer.

Meanwhile he was acquainting himself with New England, not so much in Newport as in Boston, to which the family moved in 1864,

Harvard Square as Henry James knew it in the 1860s.

The home in Newport, at the corner of Spring Street and Lee Avenue, where the James family lived 1862–63.

and in Cambridge, where two years later the parents as well as William, Henry and Alice went to live, in a tranquil, tree-shaded area (20 Quincy Street). Garth and Robertson had left after the war in an unsuccessful attempt to operate a plantation in Florida.

However unenthusiastic about the study of law, young Henry found Cambridge and Harvard delightful in themselves, 'as "American" and above all as suffused with New England colour' as he 'could possibly have wished'. His first story to be published, 'A Tragedy of Error', appeared anonymously in the *Continental Monthly* of February 1864. Later in that year he again appeared anonymously, as a commentator on books in the *North American Review*. Another tale, 'The Story of a Year', came out in March 1865, under the author's name. This was a topical story of the Civil War. The earlier tale in its European setting had hinted at the future James, but the later one illustrated what a British writer of the time was to say: that the American Civil War seemed to have been fought for the convenience

(*Far left*) Charles Eliot Norton.

(*Left*) Henry James, a portrait by John La Farge.

(*Below*) James Russell Lowell.

of novelists who wanted a plausible reason for separating their fictional lovers.

The *North American Review*, which had welcomed James to its pages, had recently taken on new life under the editorship of two of his friends, the poet James Russell Lowell and the art critic Charles Eliot Norton. But James's best friend of those Boston and Cambridge years – who was to remain staunchly so throughout James's life – was William Dean Howells. The writer from the Ohio frontier had been the American Consul at Venice during the Civil War, and after a brief time in New York had settled in Boston, home of the *Atlantic Monthly*, to which he had been a contributor. James T. Fields appointed him assistant editor in 1866, and five years later he became chief editor (until 1881), often publishing the work of Henry James. In the late 1860s, the two young men frequently took long conver-sational walks together. Howells, whose literary interests were wide ranging, also became a close friend of that utterly different kind of writer, Mark Twain.

Henry found his most intense personal attachments, however, with-in his family. His brother William once said of him, 'He is a native of the James family, and has no other country.' The mother impressed everyone by her quietness, which went along with a good-humoured firmness. The father, as remembered by Ralph Waldo Emerson's son Edward, was the centre of this 'most interesting, brilliant, original, and affectionate' family. 'He was of medium height, limped along on his

Trafalgar Square, with Morley's Hotel, where James stayed on his arrival in England in 1869 – 'a vague ruddy spot in the general immensity'.

wooden leg with some activity, but his mind and wit were most active and his temperament sympathetic.' Yet there were disturbances amid all the family liveliness and gaiety. William had his breakdown, Henry suffered from his 'obscure hurt', and Alice was ill both physically and nervously.

Henry hadn't yet published any volumes when he made his first solitary trip to Europe in 1869, but he had written numerous short stories and literary articles which continued to appear in the *Atlantic* and other leading journals. He also kept on writing reviews (still unsigned) for the *Nation*, dealing with new books by such different kinds of authors as Anthony Trollope, George Eliot, Walt Whitman, Charles Dickens and Francis Parkman. Indeed, he was to become a far more prolific writer than his father, whose fifteen publications were mostly pamphlets. The thirteenth of them, *The Secret of Swedenborg*, prompted Howells to remark that its author had kept the secret.

When James made his 1869 voyage to Europe, stopping first in England, he had a beard, with moustache, which he had worn for several years and would keep until the end of the century. Long after that arrival in England, he recalled the rainy evening on which he went from Euston Station to Morley's Hotel in Trafalgar Square:

It [the trip through London] was not lovely – in fact it was rather horrible; but as I move again through dusky, tortuous miles, in the greasy four-wheeler to which my luggage had compelled me to commit myself, I recognize the first step in an imitation of which the subsequent stages were to abound in pleasant things. It is a kind of humiliation in a great city not to know where you are going, and Morley's Hotel was then, to my imagination, only a vague ruddy spot in the general immensity. The immensity was the great fact, and that was a charm; the miles of housetops and viaducts, the complication of junctions and signals through which the train made its way to the station had already given me the scale. . . . Morley's Hotel proved indeed to be a ruddy spot; brilliant, in my recollection, is the coffee-room fire, the sense that in the stupendous city this, at any rate for the hour, was a shelter and a point of view.

Soon after settling in Half Moon Street, near the Piccadilly end, James went off on pilgrimages to Oxford, Tintern Abbey, Lincoln and other places of literary and historical attraction. Occasional remonstrances came from Quincy Street about his expenses, which the family was paying, but neither they nor illness dimmed his pleasure in seeing Europe again.

Henry James Sr – 'the look of a broker, and the brains and heart of a Pascal'. (W. E. Channing)

A view near Tewkesbury, from Henry James's sketchbook.

(*Above left*) William Morris – 'a noble and delightful poet'. (*Letters*)

(*Above right*) George Eliot – 'in this vast ugliness resides a most powerful beauty'. (*Letters*)

Suffering from constipation, James spent three weeks at a thermal sanatorium at Malvern. He had earlier met William Morris, Dante Gabriel Rossetti and John Ruskin, and now after his return to London he was presented to George Eliot, whom Minny Temple had especially wanted him to see: 'She is magnificently ugly – deliciously hideous', he wrote to his father.

She had a low forehead, a dull grey eye, a vast pendulous nose, a huge mouth full of uneven teeth and a chin and jawbone *qui n'en finissent pas*. . . . Now in this vast ugliness resides a most powerful beauty which, in a very few minutes steals forth and charms the mind, so that you end, as I ended, in falling in love with her. Yes behold me in love with this great horse-faced bluestocking.

James left England in May and spent the summer in Switzerland, which this time disappointed him. It was all raw nature, and what one should seek in Europe was 'Nature refined and transmitted into art.' The country lacked the art galleries and the fabled churches whose paintings glowed above the winking votive candles, all of which he was soon to find in Italy, particularly in Venice, Florence and Rome.

On this tour, Rome excited him more than any other place. It was on a second visit to Florence, later to become a city of his heart, that his digestive affliction recurred. He went via southern France to Paris and London, returning for more therapy at Malvern.

The women there he found dowdy and devoid of genuine charm, as he explained in a letter to William mentioning his cousin Minny and their friend Marion ('Clover') Hooper, later to become Mrs Henry Adams. Yet, despite all the faults of the women at Malvern, they were 'well enough'. But he revolted 'from their dreary deathly want of – what shall I call it? – Clover Hooper has it – intellectual grace – Minny Temple has it – moral spontaneity.' This letter was written on 8 March 1870, the very day Minny Temple died of tuberculosis – an event that signified, as Henry noted years later, both for William and himself, 'the end of our youth'.

Long afterwards William James, perhaps remembering Minny, took over from a Scottish philosopher the idea that American girls were 'bottled lightning'. To Henry James, definitely thinking of Minny, the American girl was 'the heiress of all the ages'.

(*Above left*) Dante Gabriel Rossetti. His pictures, James said, were 'all large, fanciful portraits of women ... narrow, special, monotonous, but with lots of beauty and power'. (*Letters*)

(*Above right*) John Ruskin – 'he has been scared back by the grim face of reality into the world of unreason and illusion'. (*Letters*)

After coming back home in the spring of 1870, James visited familiar New England sites and continued his writing career. William in a letter to his brother Robertson, who after the Florida failure had gone to the West with Wilky, said that Henry would probably return to Europe to live, because his taste for it 'will prevent his ever getting thoroughly reconciled to this country'.

In 1871 the *Atlantic* serialized what is technically Henry James's first novel, *Watch and Ward*, though it was not brought out as a book until seven years later. It is a story of Boston and its manners and is very light James indeed. His shorter work, 'A Passionate Pilgrim', first published in instalments in the *Atlantic* in 1871, was a story of an American abroad, pointing towards James's later use of the 'international theme'.

At the Quincy Street house, James's hunger for Europe became acute, and when Alice was sent abroad by her parents, with her Aunt Kate (Catherine Walsh) as a companion, Henry offered to escort the ladies. In order to pay back the money advanced to him by his father, he arranged to write travel essays for the *Nation*, which were later (1875) published in book form as *Transatlantic Sketches*.

The 1872 tour began in May. Henry took his sister and aunt to England, then to various places on the Continent. But Alice was often confined to bed fighting her neurasthenia, and eventually Aunt Kate grew restless. In the autumn, Henry dutifully accompanied the ladies back to England, where they sailed for home – but he remained, not to return to America until the late summer of 1874.

His writings for various American magazines supported him in these years, while he not only visited familiar places, but also The Netherlands and Belgium. He spent much time in London, Paris, Rome, and Florence. In Rome, he became addicted to riding horseback in the countryside, usually with American women who lived in the Italian capital. One of the most prominent of these was Sarah Butler, who had married a Philadelphia doctor and became the mother of Owen Wister, author of the celebrated novel of the American West, *The Virginian*. Sarah Butler Wister was the daughter of the English actress Fanny Kemble, to whom James in the course of time was indebted for much amusing conversation, some of it containing the seeds of stories which blossomed in his fiction. Another companion on those rides in the Campagna, Elizabeth ('Lizzie') Boott, was the daughter of a Europeanized American, Francis Boott, a friend who was to appear, at least in outward aspect, as a character in *The Portrait of a Lady* (1881).

In Florence, James was visited by his brother William, who was making his first trip to Italy after another of his breakdowns. Henry wasn't a full-time companion, for in the mornings his writing claimed all his attention. Antagonism, however faintly expressed, existed

Robertson James in 1891.

to harry's room where I sit
by the pungent wood fire writing this letter
which I did not expect to begin
till the afternoon, while he just
at this moment is rising from
the table where his quill has
been busily scratching away at the
last pages of his Turgenieff arti-
cle, comes to warm his legs and
puts on another log, thus do I
catch his outline.
He says I
don't do
justice
to his
beard,
which I
regret to
say since the
brilliantine regime has become

this is the short wooden jacket which ... to comfort in

Queen's Hotel Chester. May 23d
dearest Mother.

The above is a feeble sketch of the posture
& circumstances of your exiled daughter.
She sits before a great bow-window, looking
out into an elegant & verdurous garden,
the ivy creeps and clambers in along
the edges of the casement, the birds make

between the brothers, an antagonism which, despite a great deal of affection, manifested itself chiefly in William's candid and sometimes acid criticism of his brother's fiction (he had more respect for Henry's literary essays and travel sketches). William wanted to go to Rome, uprooting the reluctant Henry, who had discovered that Florence was an excellent place to write in. But he once again found it possible to work in Rome. Then William was beset by chills and fever and returned to Florence, with Henry obliged to follow. William's health improved, but Henry now fell ill, and though he soon recovered, he suffered from annoying headaches as long as his brother was there. William returned home and, after a difficult readjustment, realized that he must find himself in America.

Henry too felt that he had a duty to try living in his homeland and, though sceptical of the outcome, he went back 'with very loyal inten-
tions'. While in Florence he had begun the novel which was to be his

Letters home were often enlivened by sketches. (*Left*) Henry stooping to put another log on the fire, drawn by William James. (*Right*) Henry's impression of Alice during their tour in 1872.

35

John Hay, the friend who arranged a commission for James to write travel articles for the *New York Tribune*.

Emile Zola, a prominent member of the circle of French writers James knew in Paris; portrait by Edouard Manet.

first published in book form, and he resumed writing it at 111 East Twenty-fifth Street in New York City, where he 'spent a bright, cold, unremunerative, uninteresting winter, finishing *Roderick Hudson* and writing for the *Nation*. (It was these two tasks that kept me alive.)' But Henry had been infected by what he called the European virus. He 'very soon decided what was the real issue of [his] experiment': Europe still enchanted him, and in 1875 he made his Great Decision. He was thirty-two years old, and he would settle in Paris. He could expect royalties from his first two books, *A Passionate Pilgrim and Other Tales* and *Transatlantic Sketches*, both published in that year, and he obtained an advance from the *Atlantic*, which was serializing *Roderick Hudson*. Also, through his friend John Hay, who had been one of Lincoln's secretaries and was now an editorial writer for the *New York Tribune*, James received a commission to write travel articles for that paper. On 20 October he sailed for Liverpool, and soon he was in Paris.

In November *Roderick Hudson* was published in Boston. It is the story of a young American painter who goes to Rome, behaves foolishly, declines, and meets a mysterious death in the Swiss Alps.

(*Far left*) Gustave Flaubert. James found him 'simple, honest, kindly, and touchingly inarticulate'.

(*Left*) Ivan Turgenev, the great Russian novelist for whom James retained a lifelong admiration and affection.

An unsigned review in the *Atlantic* said that James could now be counted 'among the keenest literary artists in English and American fields'. The novel had 'a singularly perfect evenness of execution'. The anonymous notice in the *North American Review*, perhaps by James's Roman friend, Mrs Wister, was more sharply critical, though it found the last two chapters were of high excellence: 'The story has the immense merit of rising to a climax at the end.'

In Paris James had taken an apartment on the Right Bank near the Place Vendôme, on a street that began at the rue de Rivoli. He met Ivan Turgenev, whom he considered one of the world's greatest novelists; Turgenev spoke excellent English, and the two could converse in either that language or in French. Turgenev took his new friend to meet the leading French writers such as Gustave Flaubert, who received the Russian and the American wearing 'a long colloquial dressing gown'; James found that there was 'something simple, honest, kindly, and touchingly inarticulate about him'. James also made the acquaintance of Flaubert's young disciple, Guy de Maupassant, and of Edmond de Goncourt, Emile Zola, Alphonse Daudet and other French literary men, whom he met on numerous occasions. For all his admiration, however, he eventually found them rather limited, preferring style to morality.

James felt that in Paris – despite some small participation not only in literary circles, but also in society – he would 'be an eternal outsider'. In December 1876 he crossed to England, without regrets, though as he wrote to his mother, 'anyone who has ever lived in Paris will always have a corner of affection for it in his heart and will often go back'.

Henry James in London, a cartoon by Max Beerbohm.

Visions of poverty – an illustration for James's novella 'In the Cage'.

James's connection with the *Tribune* had dissolved, but he remained in England, continuing to write fiction. In 1877 he brought out his novel *The American*, which had appeared in serial form in the *Atlantic*. He had begun it in Paris, and the story revolves round a visiting American somewhat allegorically named Christopher Newman, who has come to that city to see Europe and to obtain a wife. Though the situation was a familiar one in French literature of the nineteenth century, James lent it novelty by making his quester an American.

In the novel, the aristocratic Bellegardes snobbishly intervene to prevent the marriage of the 'self-made' Newman to the daughter of the family, an attractive young widow, whom they force into a nunnery. Newman discovers proof of a hidden murder in the family, but when he threatens to expose the Bellegardes, they defy him. He destroys the evidence against them, as they had known he would, for he is a 'decent' American. Here again James makes use of his 'international theme'; this is one story among several dealing with the defeat of an American by Europeans. Years later, James came to believe that *The American* was really improbable and that the Bellegardes would not have turned away an American millionaire.

Through the winter of 1877–78, James rejoiced in London. He was lonely at first but was soon invited into society. He relished the blearing fogs and even the almost endless drizzle, and often walked along the pavements, past the unending reddish-brick houses, finding all of it enchanting. The one element of London life that distressed him was the bleak poverty. In Italy the poor had been picturesque; in England they lived in grey misery. James would eventually write stories with this poverty as part of the background, notably the novel *The Princess Casamassima* (1886) and the novella 'In the Cage' (1898).

James's friend Henry Adams gave him a letter of introduction to the literary connoisseur Richard Monckton Milnes, Lord Houghton, and James began to move in a more exclusive society than in Paris. At one dinner party at Houghton's, for example, he met W.E. Gladstone and Lord Tennyson. He was given (at the instigation of the historian John Lothrop Motley) an honorary membership in one of London's finest clubs, the Athenaeum, and he took rooms at 3 Bolton Street, just off Piccadilly (like his former residence in near-by Half Moon Street). 'I have *lived* much there', he wrote, years later, of the Bolton Street lodgings, 'felt much, thought much, produced much; the little shabby furnished apartment ought to be sacred to me. I came to London as a complete stranger, and today I know much too many people. *J'y suis absolument comme chez moi.*'

In 1878 his novel *The Europeans* presented a light-comedy view of two Europeanized Americans, a young man and his sister, a baroness, and of the amusing, ironic, and international complications that follow upon their encounter with their American cousins who live in

Jacket illustration for the pirate
English edition of *The American*

a Boston suburb. It was probably this novel (despite its brevity first
printed in two volumes) which figures in a ruefully comic story James
told about himself in the uncompleted part of his autobiography, *The
Middle Years*, posthumously published in 1917. In 1879 James's
friend Mrs Richard Greville had brought him to Surrey to visit George
Eliot and George Henry Lewes and had also taken along a two-
volume James novel, which she said her host and hostess should read.

Autograph manuscript of the opening page of *The Europeans*.

When James and Mrs Greville were leaving, Lewes went with them to their carriage, then suddenly asked James to wait a moment. James returned to the front door, into which Lewes had darted, to reappear in a moment brandishing the books and shouting, 'Take them, please, please, away, away!' The mortified James convinced himself across the years that Lewes and George Eliot hadn't realized whose novel they were refusing.

In his late-period autobiographical writings James included many personal 'touches' of this kind, but he never revealed the deeper truths about himself, nor has any material about them emerged. Concerning his possible sexual experiences there is no information, no real hint of physical relationships. The closest to any kind of evidence is in two recollections, one by Sir Edmund Gosse, the other by Sir Hugh Walpole, whose accounts complement one another. 'He spoke of standing on the pavement of a city', Gosse recalled, 'in the dusk, and of gazing upwards across the misty street, watching, watching, for the lighting of a lamp in a window on the third storey.' For hours he stood there, weeping in the rain. Walpole told essentially the same tale, which he may have heard from Gosse, placing it in a foreign town in James's youth.

Max Beerbohm's caricature, *A Rage of Wonderment*, hints at the mature Henry James's powerful imagination – the observations and experiences which provided what he called the '*données*' of his novels.

Afternoon on the Pincian Hill in Rome, described by James in *Daisy Miller*.

We have no further clue. Many commentators have suggested that James's youthful accident may have made him impotent. Some investigators have tried to sniff out homosexuality in James's often seemingly fervent friendships, later in his life, with young writers and artists; but as his masterly biographer Leon Edel has said, 'The evidence is tenuous.' Furthermore, both W. Somerset Maugham and Stephen Spender have reported that Walpole told them of offering himself to James, who replied, 'I can't, I can't.'

Looking over the known facts, others have wondered whether Minny Temple's early death might not have made him a voluntary celibate. Writing to his mother after Minny's death, James said, 'It comes home to me with irresistible power, the sense of how much I knew her and how much I loved her' – but this could have been just an intense family affection. At that time he had also written to his brother William, 'Every one was supposed, I believe, to be more or less in love with her: others may answer for themselves: I never was, and yet I had the great satisfaction that I enjoyed *pleasing* her almost as if I had been.' That she remained in his mind and heart, however, is witnessed by her later appearances in his fiction, notably as Isabel Archer in *The Portrait of a Lady* (1881) and as Milly Theale in *The Wings of the Dove* (1902).

Another kind of American girl appeared in James's short novel *Daisy Miller* (1878), which sold better than any of his previous books. While he was in Rome in 1877, on one of those 'vacations' which brought him almost annually to the Continent, an American friend with whom he used to go riding in the Campagna – apparently Alice Bartlett – told him that during the previous winter an American girl, 'a child of nature and freedom', had provoked the disapproval of Anglo-American society in Rome because she went about unchaperoned with an Italian 'of vague identity'.

Daisy Miller is told from the point of view of a young American in Europe, Frederick Winterbourne, who first meets Daisy in Switzerland and admires her cheerful spontaneity. Later, seeing her with her friend Giovanelli in different parts of Rome, Winterbourne gravely disapproves of her conduct although he continues to treat her courteously. When, on a night of thin moon above 'the dusky circle of the Colosseum', he sees Daisy there with Giovanelli, he warns her about Roman fever, a rather frequent affliction of that time, brought about by the cool Roman nights (James's friend Edith Wharton wrote, years later, a story called 'Roman Fever'). Daisy contracts the fever and dies. Giovanelli tells Winterbourne that Daisy was 'innocent', and Winterbourne leaves for Switzerland, where his aunt suggests that if he had loved Daisy, she would have returned his love. Winterbourne is one of the many among James's male characters who observe rather than participate.

An illustration from the *Cornhill Magazine* for *Washington Square*.

James's social life intensified in those years; in London during the winter of 1879 he dined out on 109 nights. In the late 1870s he wrote mostly short fiction, including the stories 'Longstaff's Marriage', 'An International Episode', 'The Pension Beaurepas' and 'The Diary of a Man of Fifty', all interesting studio sketches of an artist growing in craftsmanship.

In 1880, James turned out one of his finest works of fiction, *Washington Square*, incorporating memories of his birthsite in the grimly forceful story of a tyrannous doctor who spoils the lives of his daughter and her suitor. It was based on an anecdote of Fanny Kemble's; James transplanted the scene from England to America. He had dealt with another American topic in his *Hawthorne*, in the English Men of Letters series, which he completed in Paris in the autumn of 1879. Published in December of that year, the little study was favourably received in England, but not in the United States, where it appeared the following year. Even Howells, who sent James his anonymous *Atlantic* review of the book, jibbed somewhat at the reference to Hawthorne as 'exquisitely provincial'.

James was reminded of America again when he met Constance Fenimore Woolson in Florence in 1880. A native of Ohio, a grand-niece of James Fenimore Cooper, and herself a writer, the thirty-nine-year-old bluestocking aroused somewhat unusual sympathy in James, who took her to the galleries and gave her vivid lectures on the paint-ings and statues. But apparently he kept aloof from any deeply personal relationship. He wrote to his Aunt Kate, 'Constance is old-maidish, deaf, and "intense"; but a good little woman and a perfect lady.' They were to meet often again.

Returning to London in the spring of 1880, Henry James saw his brother William for the first time in five years. Though William had married a pretty Boston school-teacher, Alice Howe Gibbens, in 1878, he now travelled to Europe alone, still plagued by fatigue and eye trouble. He didn't care much about meeting Henry's London friends, whom he would probably never see again. Henry was sur-prised to find his brother still the victim of 'nervousness and insta-bility' and wrote to Quincy Street that William took 'himself, and his nerves, and his physical condition too hard and too consciously'. When William was there, Henry apparently had a recurrence of his

A sketch of himself by William James.

The house on the Riva degli Schiavoni where James lived during his stay in Venice in 1881.

headaches: soon after the older brother had left for the Continent, Henry wrote that he was just recovering from them.

In February 1881 he too crossed the Channel and went for his longest stay in Venice. He took a room on the Riva degli Schiavoni (number 4161) overlooking the 'far-shining lagoon', where 'Palladio's church, San Giorgio Maggiore, had a faint, shimmering, airy, watery pink; the bright sea-light seems to flush with it, and the pale whitish green of lagoon and canal to drink it in.' Like so many pilgrims to Venice before and after, James in the evenings often sat outdoors at Florian's *caffè* in the Piazza San Marco, listening to the music of its little orchestra and watching the Venetians and the tourists amble past. In the afternoons he worked steadily on a novel, which was being serialized by *Macmillan's Magazine* and the *Atlantic Monthly* and was to be published as a book later that year.

(*Overleaf*) The Piazzetta di San Marco, looking towards San Giorgio Maggiore, 'a faint, shimmering, airy, watery pink'. (*Letters*)

45

The Boott family in the garden of the Villa Castellani. In the foreground, Francis Boott and his daughter Lizzie; in the background, her husband Frank Duveneck and her nurse, Mary Ann Shenstone.

This, his first major novel, was *The Portrait of a Lady*, centred in the adventures of an American girl in Europe, the attractive and energetic Isabel Archer whose last name, as commentators have pointed out, links her to Diana (Artemis), the chaste moon-goddess who hunted with bow and arrow. In presenting her expatriate relatives in England, notably her sick cousin Ralph, James drew a careful portrait of well-meaning Americans abroad; but he was aware that there were other kinds of Americans in Europe as well, such as the calculating dilettante Gilbert Osmond and his American-born former mistress, Madame Merle. Osmond's villa above Florence is modelled upon the Castellani, belonging to Francis Boott, from whom much of Osmond's external character is also borrowed, though to it has been added a smooth villainy all his own. Boott's daughter Lizzie served James as the prototype of Pansy, the offspring of Osmond and Mme Merle, whom Isabel believes to be the child of an earlier marriage.

In the novel Isabel, prompted by Mme Merle, is drawn into a sterile and increasingly unhappy marriage with Osmond. Eventually she discovers the true parentage of Pansy and perceives that Mme Merle's solicitude and encouragement have all the time been aimed at assuring Osmond's comfort and her daughter's future. Returning alone to visit her relatives in England, the disillusioned Isabel encounters an earlier suitor who holds out to her once again a promise of the warmth, understanding and goodwill that are totally missing from her marriage; but she renounces this chance for starting afresh and returns to her husband, partly out of loyalty to the innocent Pansy, whom she now feels she must protect, but also, as she explains to an American woman-friend, because 'One must accept one's deeds. I married him before all the world; I was perfectly free; it was impossible to do anything more deliberate.'

Isabel's return, as James himself confides in his notebooks, 'is the climax and termination of the story'. In its renunciation of self-interest, it represents a moral triumph.

Only a cosmopolitan American like James could have written a novel of such scope and complexity, one that involves Americans of such varied character and that ranges so easily from England to Florence and Rome. Isabel, who is largely based upon James's memories of Minny Temple, is in all ways a remarkable character. But so, indeed, is almost everyone else in the novel. Osmond is a superb portrait of a self-centred aesthete, capable of occasional malignity. And it is interesting to see, as one may still do today, the Antica Mattei, the palazzo James selected for Osmond's residence in Rome: its very appearance is sinister. Although the book is a variation on the 'international theme' – for here the difficulties are generated not by Europeans but by Europeanized Americans – the themes of adultery and treachery were to reappear in James's fiction, most notably in his late-period works *The Wings of the Dove* and *The Golden Bowl*.

Before *The Portrait of a Lady* reached the bookshops in 1881, James had again crossed the Atlantic westwards after stopping briefly in England to see his sister Alice, who was there with her friend Katherine Loring as a nurse-companion. Back in Massachusetts, he stayed first at the Quincy Street house, where he sadly noted how much his mother had aged. Subsequently, he moved to the Brunswick Hotel in Boston, where at a marble-top table on a bleak November day he put down in a notebook his deepest thoughts on the best place for him to live: 'My choice is the old world – my choice, my need, my life.' Fortunately, he tells himself, he had made the decision years before. He wouldn't at the moment note his impressions of America, which were considerably sharper when he was away from them in Europe.

Now, 'Heaven forgive me! I feel as if my time were terribly wasted here.' He went to New York for a while, but it seemed little better.

In both Boston and New York, interruptions 'in the *morning*' were 'intolerable', he wrote in his notebook. The morning didn't have 'the social sanctity' that it had in England. In the United States there were constant intrusions, social and otherwise: 'I have had all sorts of things to do, chiefly not profitable to recall.' He thought, by contrast, of the English manors:

those delicious old houses, in the long August days, in the south of England air, on the soil over which so much has passed and out of which so much has come, rose before me like a series of visions. I thought of a thousand things; what becomes of the things one thinks of at these times? They are not lost, we must hope; they drop back into the mind again, and they enrich and embellish it.

In this passage we see not only the novelist's grasp of atmosphere and meanings, but even an anticipation of Freud's theories about the operations of the unconscious.

He had for some time considered writing for the stage, and discussed this possibility in a long notebook entry which seems to date from the end of 1881. He had previously held himself back from attempts at play-writing, but now looking at the drama, he found it 'the ripest of all arts, the one to which one must bring most of the acquired as well as most of the natural'; while he was waiting to approach it, he had been studying the art closely 'and clearing off my field'. He believed that he had mastered the French theatre of the time: the works of Dumas, Sardou and Augier. And he had been strongly moved by the brilliant performances of his old schoolfellow, Constant Coquelin. But James had been so involved in 'writing things for which I needed to be paid from month to month' that he hadn't time to attempt the theatre.

Washington, which he visited for the first time in early January 1882, seemed superficial. The enormous, long-haired, and overdressed Oscar Wilde, who was being entertained everywhere, struck James as 'an unclean beast' and a 'fatuous cad'. James enjoyed the Henry Adamses, however; as noted earlier, Adams was married to the Marion ('Clover') Hooper whom the novelist had admired in his youth. A little more than two years later she killed herself after the death of her father, whom she loved with intensity, suggesting the daughter-father attachment in James's late novel, *The Golden Bowl*.

While he was in Washington he received a telegram from Quincy Street saying that his mother was critically ill; he returned to Cambridge at once, but she had died before his arrival. As he later wrote in his notebook, 'It is impossible for me to say – to begin to say – all that has gone down into the grave with her. She was our life, she was the house, she was the keystone of the arch. . . . She was patience, she was wisdom, she was exquisite maternity.'

Henry James's mother in old age.

Henry James at the age of 39; a wood engraving by Timothy Cole which appeared in the November 1882 issue of *Century Magazine*.

Bostonian aestheticism proving immune to the charms of Oscar Wilde.

Boston Common as James would have seen it in 1882.

Henry James moved back to Boston, to a house on Beacon Hill, where he spent several months grieving over his mother. He occupied his writing time with a dramatization of *Daisy Miller*, to which he gave a 'happy ending', but the New York producers who looked at the manuscript of the play turned it down as too 'literary'. James noted that, in their manner of rejecting his play, the proprietors of the Madison Square Garden Theatre 'behaved like asses and sharpers combined; this episode, by the way, would make a brilliant chapter in a realistic novel'.

Returning to London in May, James stopped briefly in Ireland to visit the land of his ancestors. As on two subsequent visits, he found little there to please him. And even London now seemed a bit dull. A trip to the Continent resulted in *A Little Tour in France*, serialized in the *Atlantic* in 1883–84, and brought out as a book in 1885. Meanwhile,

A late portrait of Henry James Sr, by Frank Duveneck.

in the autumn of 1882, the year in which James's mother had died, his father sank into a fatal illness – 'the little fat, rosy Swedenborgian amateur', as William Ellery Channing described him, with 'the look of a broker, and the brains and heart of a Pascal'.

Once again James arrived too late for the death of a beloved parent. This time he was on a transatlantic liner bound for New York; his father was buried the day before the ship docked. From Europe, William wrote a letter which was also too late. Henry took it out to their father's grave and standing there on an icy Sunday he read the letter aloud. It ended, 'Good-night, my sacred old father. If I don't see you again – Farewell! a blessed farewell!'

In another letter, written to his wife four days before his father died, William James made plain his feelings about England, a country 'all clogged and stuffed with the great load of superfluities, the great

(*Above*) John Singer Sargent, by Beerbohm.

(*Above right*) The seashore at Bournemouth, where James stayed with Alice and where his earlier acquaintance with Stevenson deepened into friendship.

rubbish-heap and sweepings of centuries that she drags after her, smeared in the fog and smoke'. A month later, however, his mood had changed. England still did not 'agree with' him, he wrote, yet rather ruefully he felt he must escape to Paris in order to save his life because he found himself liking the English

people more and more. Of all the *Kunst-produkte* of this globe the exquisitely and far-fetchedly fashioned structure called the English Race and Temperament is the most precious. . . . A poor Frenchman would behold with a kind of frenzy the easy and genial way in which [that structure] solves, or achieves without needing to solve, all those things which are for his unfortunate people the impossible.

In 1883 Henry returned to Europe, and once more death struck those close to him: his hapless brother Wilky died, and so did his revered friend Turgenev, whom James had seen in Paris during the Russian novelist's last illness.

But life also surged around James, for in 1883–84 the Macmillan Company in London brought out a fourteen-volume collection of his *Novels and Tales*. And new books of his kept appearing, stories and travel sketches. The novella 'Lady Barberina', written at this time, is one of James's finest applications of the 'international theme', the story of an English aristocrat whose compulsive need for society draws her American husband away from his medical research – in some ways foreshadowing F. Scott Fitzgerald's 1934 novel, *Tender is the Night*.

Robert Louis Stevenson. James was profoundly moved by the death in 1894 of 'the beloved R.L.S.' – 'he lighted up a whole side of the globe, and was himself a whole province of one's imagination'. (*Letters*)

In the middle years and second half of the 1880s, James made several trips to the Continent, chiefly to France and Italy. He had revisited France early in 1884, again meeting Edmond de Goncourt, Zola and Daudet, as well as encountering some younger writers, such as François Coppée and Pierre Loti, and the young American artist, John Singer Sargent, who in the course of time was to draw and paint him on several occasions.

During his stay in Paris in 1884, James made rather ambivalent comments on the French authors he had seen. As before, James felt that these men were narrow, yet that they were also bolder, more innovative than their English and American contemporaries. He told Howells that these writers 'do the only kind of work, today, that I respect'. He had gone to Paris three weeks earlier, 'on the principle that anything is quieter than London; but I return to the British scramble in a few days. Paris speaks to me, always, for about such a time as this; with many voices; but at the end of a month I have learned all it has to say.'

He spent the spring and summer of 1884 in London, writing, and then stayed for a few weeks at Dover. In November he had to go to Liverpool to meet his nerve-stretched sister, who was arriving from America with a nurse-companion and her own ailing sister, of whom Alice James was fiercely jealous. Henry took her to London, then down to Bournemouth. Robert Louis Stevenson was also staying

Alice James and her nurse-companion, Katherine Loring, in their sitting-room at Leamington.

at the seaside resort, and he and James – they had met earlier – became good friends and frequent correspondents during the ten years Stevenson had yet to live. Alice James spent her own remaining seven years in Leamington and London, often visited by her brother.

In 1885 James learned something that had been kept tightly secret and for many years thereafter was known to only a discreet few: the suicide of Henry Adams's wife, Clover. The grieving husband set over her anonymous grave in Rock Creek Cemetery at Washington the statue of brooding grief by Augustus Saint-Gaudens. The suicide of Clover Hooper Adams may have afforded part of the background for the story James wrote in 1886, 'The Modern Warning' (first published in 1888), in which a woman suicide is strongly attached to her brother. The principal theme of the tale, however, is international antagonisms, represented here by England against America. The

Alice James during her years in England.

story ends with the possibility that the individuals representing each country may become reconciled. Although not one of James's better known tales, 'The Modern Warning' is an interesting example of his ability to take events from life and transform them into a story so expressive of his own feelings, in this case suggesting that he wanted greater understanding and amity between the two nations themselves.

Settling again in London, James realized that, with so many homeland connections broken, he had found his true home forever: 'It is an anchorage for life.' Because his rooms in Bolton Street were small and dark, he was delighted to find a large fourth-floor flat at 34 De Vere Gardens, Kensington, with a fine view across the scribble of London rooftops and trees. He took a long lease on his new quarters and installed himself early in 1886.

34 De Vere Gardens, where James took a large flat in 1886.

During that same year he had brought out two new novels, *The Bostonians* and *The Princess Casamassima*. The former contains, among the principal male characters, a man who has moved to New York from the Deep South. He is in active pursuit of a young woman, Verena Tarrant, who is also being pursued by Olive Chancellor, a forerunner of members of the women's liberation movement; she wants to control Verena, the daughter of an animal-magnetism charlatan. The relationship of Olive and Verena at some levels prefigures the popular novel *Trilby*, which came out ten years later. (Oddly enough, before George du Maurier wrote *Trilby* he offered James the plot.) James's novel, far too prolix for its necessities, was in one way a farewell to America in often satiric terms. As he said in a letter to his brother William in 1886: 'All the middle part is too diffuse and insistent – far too much describing and explaining and expatiating. The whole thing is too long and dawdling.' James went on to say that since he didn't sufficiently know the milieu and the types of people he had portrayed, he had 'felt a constant pressure to make the picture substantial by thinking it out – pencilling and "shading".' He was, in any event, becoming more skilful as a prose-writer, letting language create exactly the mood of both settings and characters:

The western windows of Olive's drawing-room, looking over the water, took in the red sunsets of winter; the long, low bridge that crawled, on its staggering posts, across the Charles; the casual patches of ice and snow; the desolate suburban horizons, peeled and made bald by the rigour of the season; the general hard, cold, void of the prospect; the extrusion, at Charlestown, at Cambridge, of a few chimneys and steeples, straight, sordid tubes of factories and engine-shops, or spare, heavenward finger of the New England meeting house. There was something inexorable in the poverty of the scene, shameful in the meanness of its detail, which gave a collective impression of boards and tin and frozen earth, sheds and rotting piles, railway-lines striding flat across a thoroughfare of puddles, and tracks of the humbler, the universal horse-car, traversing obliquely this path of danger; loose fences, vacant lots, mounds of refuse, yards bestrewn with iron pipes, telegraph poles, and bare wooded backs of places. Verena thought such a view lovely, and she was by no means without excuse when, as the afternoon closed, the ugly picture was tinted with a clear, cold rosiness. The air, in its windless chill, and the faintest gradations of tone were perceptible in the sky, the west became deep and delicate, everything grew doubly distinct before taking on the dimness of evening. There were pink flushes on snow, 'tender' reflections in patches of stiffened marsh, sounds of car-bells, no longer vulgar but almost silvery, on the long bridge, lonely outlines of distant dusky undulations against the fading glow.

In such passages he caught the atmosphere of Boston, as he was to capture that of London in *The Princess Casamassima*, particularly concerning himself with the poverty which was evident on all sides, even in Mayfair. His familiarity with Dickens's works had for long given him a humanized sense of the subject, and he even visited a grim prison to see what conditions in such places were like. But many of his reviewers felt that he was too little acquainted with the revolutionists he was writing about, though most of these critics erroneously spoke of the anarchists as socialists. The reviews hurt James, and about this time he wondered whether he would be 'condemned to eternal silence'.

Later critics, however, have turned to both these novels with more approval; in the case of *The Princess Casamassima*, Leon Edel and Lionel Trilling have been particularly elucidative. That James felt a novelist didn't have to be born into the milieu he deals with, we know from his essay of 1884, 'The Art of Fiction', written for *Longman's Magazine* in answer to a lecture and pamphlet on the subject by the now-faded bestseller, Walter Besant. Besant's lecture later appeared as a book, along with James's riposte. Besant had said that 'a young lady

Sargent's intimate, sumptuous view of life in a Venetian palazzo.

brought up in a quiet country village should avoid descriptions of garrison life; a writer whose friends and personal experiences belong to what we call the lower middle class should carefully avoid intro‚ ducing his characters into Society' – statements with which James vigorously disagreed. His principal objection, however, was to Besant's claim that novels should have 'a conscious moral purpose'. James asks how the novel, 'being a picture', can 'be either moral or immoral'. James elaborates on this point, which seven years later in Oscar Wilde's aphoristic preface to *The Picture of Dorian Gray* was to be stated again, with variations: 'There is no such thing as a moral or immoral book. Books are well written, or badly written. That is all.' James's outlook was of course far less simple, and most of his fiction has an intrinsic morality.

James intended to spend only one month in Italy when he returned there in December 1886, but he remained for eight, staying seven weeks in Venice as the guest of Robert Browning's firm friend, Mrs Katherine De Kay Bronson of Boston. James lived in a guest apartment in a palace at the rear of her Casa Alvisi, at the mouth of the Grand Canal and just opposite the Church of Santa Maria della Salute. He was always to admire the view from the front balcony of the Casa Alvisi, where in 1881 he had often sat with Mrs Bronson and Robert Browning, but during the February and March of 1887 he found the 'glutinous malodorous damp' too much for him. There was even a depressingly heavy snowfall in March, with 'sinister carts in the Piazza [San Marco] and men who looked like Irishmen shovelling away snow'.

The Rialto Bridge over the Grand Canal.

61

Constance Fenimore Woolson.

'Juliana's Court' in Ca' Capella, the frontispiece to 'The Aspern Papers'.

(*Opposite*) The Palazzo Barbaro on the Grand Canal, where James stayed with his friends the Curtises, was later to serve in his fiction as the residence of Milly Theale.

He went on to Florence, where he stayed once again up in Bellos‑guardo, this time at the Villa Brichieri‑Colombi, on the hill‑slope road below the Villa Castellani, where his friends the Bootts still lived. Elizabeth Boott had recently married the German‑born American painter, Frank Duveneck. One of the guests at the Castellani was Constance Fenimore Woolson, who had leased the Brichieri but had in turn rented it to her old companion, Henry James. Later Miss Woolson moved into the Brichieri, and both writers were engaged in their day's writing in different parts of the building. The joint tenancy was a perfectly innocent one. That his companion wanted things to be otherwise is problematic, though the thought of marrying James quite possibly occurred to her; Leon Edel has suggested that James put her into 'The Aspern Papers' as the niece (or grand‑niece) of the ancient woman who greedily clutched the Aspern letters.

James in his own letters was usually silent on the score of his sharing the villa with a woman, but he told many of his correspondents that the Brichieri had a beautiful view of the roofs and towers of Florence. At the villa he wrote most of 'The Aspern Papers', that tensely dramatic story he took from two anecdotes he had heard on a single day in Florence. One of them concerned the burning of one of Byron's love‑letters, which horrified James – so reticent about his own private papers – and the other report involved the woman generally known as Claire Clairmont, friend of both Shelley and Byron, once mistress of the latter and mother of his daughter Allegra. James recorded in his notebook that a sea‑captain from Boston named Silsbee, who was a fervent admirer of Shelley, heard of the Shelley‑Byron papers and arranged to lodge in the house in Florence where they were secreted. He was correct in his assumption that Claire Clairmont would soon die and, when she did, he approached her niece about the papers. She said, 'I will give you all the letters if you marry me!' As James's informant added, 'Silsbee *court encore.*'

James moved the locale of his story out of Florence for fairly obvious reasons, and quite possibly chose Venice for its background because the twisting little sinister back‑canals appropriately suggested the convolutions of greed and villainy. For the setting of the story he borrowed the Ca' Capella on the Rio Marin. James used another aspect of Venice about a dozen years later, in the rainstorm scene in *The Wings of the Dove*, involving a quite different kind of evil. 'The Aspern Papers' has the tensions of a superior detective story, intensi‑fied by the moral problem: do the letters of a great man belong to the world, or do bargaining old women have the right to destroy them?

On his way back to London, James stayed five weeks with his friends the Daniel Curtises in Venice, at the Palazzo Barbaro on the Grand Canal, the building which was to serve as Milly Theale's residence in *The Wings of the Dove*. One of James's acquaintances at this

time was May Marcy McLellan, daughter of Abraham Lincoln's dilatory general. She had shocked fellow Americans in Italian society by writing candidly about them in an American newspaper, giving James the idea for his short novel *The Reverberator* (1888), in which he used a Parisian setting for what turns out to be a neat little comedy of manners. In another story about Americans abroad, 'A London Life' (1888), James dealt with the ferocious moralism of a girl from Virginia who, visiting her married sister in England, disapproves of that sister's love-affairs. James later referred to 'A London Life' as 'my comprehensive picture of bewildered Americanism'.

He returned to his Kensington flat late in July 1887 and there wrote his tale, 'The Lesson of the Master', in which a young writer heeds the advice of a famous author whom he meets at an English country-house party: he should avoid such entanglements as marriage, for they hamper one's writing; the older author has been forced, because of his wife and children, to turn out clever, popular books. The young man goes to the Continent for two years, writes his second novel, and returns to England to find that the wife of the 'Master' has died and that he has married again – the very girl the younger man was in love with. He reproaches the older man, who maintains that the advice was sound. This is one of James's most distinctive tales of writers and artists; to such stories he brought not only his own writing and moral experiences in relation to the craft, but also a special affection for those having artistic problems.

Grim tidings came to James at Easter-time 1888: Francis Boott's daughter Elizabeth, now Mrs Duveneck and the mother of a fifteen-month-old child, had died of pneumonia in Paris. To James, who had known from her childhood this friend of Minny Temple's, Lizzie's 'sudden death was an unspeakable shock'. He found it difficult to believe at first: 'It was the last thing I ever thought of as possible – I mean before Boott's own surrender of his earthly burden.'

Early in that year of 1888, James had begun his novel, *The Tragic Muse* (1890), whose plot, though centred in the theatre, contains sorties into painters' studios and the world of high diplomacy. It is a long and tangled story, but one that stays alive, although reviewers on both sides of the Atlantic cared little for it and, like the two preceding long novels *The Bostonians* and *The Princess Casamassima*, it didn't attract the book-buying public. But its very subject, essentially the story of the actress Miriam Rooth, points towards the interest in the theatre which James was soon to manifest. Indeed, it was to dominate his life between 1890 and 1895.

The stage beckoned to him first in the person of the actor Edward Compton, whose wife was the American actress Virginia Bateman and whose son was to become the writer Sir Compton Mackenzie. Edward Compton wrote to James suggesting that he dramatize *The*

Edward Compton as Christopher Newman in the stage version of *The American.*

Programme for Compton's production of *The American* in London, 1891.

Elizabeth Robins as Claire de Cintré in *The American*.

American, and he paid an advance of £250 on it in 1890. James apologized, in letters to various friends, for yielding to the vulgarity of modern theatre, but said that, since his books didn't sell, he needed the income which plays would probably bring him.

The American opened at Southport, near Liverpool, on 3 January 1891, and was greeted enthusiastically by its first audience. As in his unproduced dramatization of *Daisy Miller*, James created a 'happy ending' for his adaptation of *The American*: his hero is finally able to marry the charming young widow, Claire de Cintré (in a later version,

Part of an adverse review of *The American*: 'Mr James has given us a play which is more than sufficiently descriptive, and far from vigorously dramatic.'

to make the little comedy of manners altogether untragic, Claire's brother is not killed in a duel as he was in both the novel and the earlier version of the play).

After Compton toured with *The American* for some months he decided to take it into London. Most of the critics wrote unfavourably of the play, which they thought spoiled James's novel by adding melodramatic and farcical elements. Compton, in his long overcoat with large buttons on it, was the broad caricature of an American. James had even written down for Compton the pronunciations he should use, such as *awf* for *off*. And the reviewers were rather harsh with the young American actress, Elizabeth Robins, who became a friend of James's. She had successfully played intense Ibsen heroines, such as Nora Tesman and Hedda Gabler, on the London stage: the critics felt that she was too energetic in the role of the fundamentally passive Claire.

The Prince of Wales helped keep the play afloat by attending one of the performances, an event that was used for publicity, but *The American* lasted for only seventy nights, and James made little money out of it. Yet he was still determined to triumph in the theatre. In 1892 he wrote a play which interested the American producer, Augustin Daly, who had built a theatre in London for his star, Ada Rehan. The little comedy, which James later published as *Disengaged*, was accepted

James's list of alternative titles for his play *Disengaged*.

by Daly, who wanted to call it *Mrs Jasper's Way*, emphasizing the role Ada Rehan would take. Scenery and costumes were designed, and work had started on them, but in spite of the many changes in the script which James made at Daly's request, the play never came to life: James was appalled at the first reading, at which the actors ground out their lines perfunctorily. After some correspondence with the producer, James angrily withdrew the play, and Daly and Ada Rehan turned to other dramas. James soon made another attempt to capture the London stage, with *Guy Domville*, written in 1893 but not produced until 1895.

All during this period he kept busy with shorter fiction, and in 1893 the results were published in two volumes, *The Private Life* and *The Real Thing and Other Stories*. The title story of the latter volume is an amusing investigation of the role that art plays in relation to reality: a painter hires a senior army officer and his wife as models for figures in high society, but discovers that they are too inflexible, too 'unreal', to work with him, so he engages models from the lower classes who can adapt themselves to the mood of the paintings. In the book named for the story 'The Private Life' – which deals with a writer who has two identities and a politician who has none – the most highly regarded tale is 'Owen Wingrave', which has been made into an opera by Benjamin Britten and is one of James's outstanding stories of the supernatural. It concerns a young man who refuses to follow family

Peter Pears (*right foreground*), Heather Harper, and John Shirley-Quirk in the final scene of Benjamin Britten's opera *Owen Wingrave*, first produced for television in 1971.

tradition and become a soldier. Challenged by a girl who disbelieves his assertion that he spent a harrowing night in a haunted room, he returns to it, and is found there in the early morning, mysteriously dead, and looking like a soldier.

James had in this period encountered death more intimately than ever before. His mother and father had died while he was away from them, but he was present during the last stages of his sister's fatal illness (cancer) in London in 1892. The brilliant, nerve-broken Alice had kept a remarkable diary during the last three years of her life. It was full of personal and family matters, as well as comments on public events and personages of the time. After Alice's death, her nurse-companion, Katherine Peabody Loring, arranged for the printing of most of the diary in an edition limited to four copies. Henry, who was horrified at the intimacies revealed, apparently destroyed his copy. William's eventually went to the repository of manuscripts and rare books in the Houghton Library at Harvard. In 1934 a mutilated version of the journal was published by the daughter of Robertson James, who turned the book into a tribute to the unrecognized James brothers, Robertson and Wilky. It was not until 1964, under the editorship of Leon Edel, that readers could examine a complete-as-possible version of *The Diary of Alice James*.

During the first half of the 1890s, James continued to make short trips to France, Switzerland, and Italy, usually staying at the Palazzo

Aubrey Beardsley's design on the back cover of the *Yellow Book* for April 1894, featuring James's story 'The Death of the Lion'.

Barbaro with his friends the Curtises. Once (1892) he was the guest of an old friend who had rented the Palazzo for the summer: Isabella Gardner, usually known as Mrs Jack Gardner, the notable and lively art-collector from Boston.

A later visit to Venice was a sad one. In January 1894, Constance Fenimore Woolson, who had rented a Venetian palazzo, was found on the small pavement beside it, dying. She had been ill, and a second-storey window was open. When James received the news in London he was severely shocked and planned to attend the funeral in Rome, where Constance Woolson was to be buried, as she had wished, in the Protestant Cemetery, near the graves of Keats and Shelley.

James had already booked passage when he learned that Miss Woolson's death was probably suicide. This jarred him, and he cancelled his plans. He later wrote to a friend that he believed Constance Woolson's action was one of 'irresponsible, delirious insanity', intensified by her illness and fever. In March, however, he went to Italy to help the dead woman's sister and niece to sort out the hodge-podge of personal papers. It was a five weeks' task. Afterwards, he stayed on in Venice for a while, but the noisy throngs of summer tourists appalled him: 'They are all "our" people – yours and mine', he wrote to an American friend, 'and they dis-Italianize this dear patient old Italy. . . . The accent of Massachusetts rings up and down the Grand Canal and the bark of Chicago disturbs the siesta.'

Before leaving England, James had written 'The Death of the Lion', the story of a middle-aged author just coming into recognition who is taken up, much to his bewilderment and unhappiness, by an aristo-cratic hostess who, with her heavy social demands upon him, crushes him to death and doesn't care a whit that the manuscript he has recently completed is lost. This tale appeared in the new journal of the aesthetes, the *Yellow Book*, in 1894, and so did a long story James wrote in

Venice after the Woolson ordeal. 'The Coxon Fund' is the tale of a somewhat Coleridge-like philosopher who is a brilliant conversationalist but totally impractical – and an alcoholic. He accepts as his due from society a fund which will free him to create, a fund whose donation leaves another character in the story impoverished. And then, ironically, the man to whom the money was given collapses into an easy life and his drunkenness. Both these *Yellow Book* stories were included in a volume, *Terminations*, in the following year, 1895.

After returning to England, James became involved in plans to produce *Guy Domville*, the play for which he had vehement hopes. After Edward Compton rejected it, James sold it to the popular actor-manager George Alexander. During the rehearsal period, in December 1894, James received word that his friend Stevenson had died in Samoa at the age of forty-four. James was stricken with sadness, but kept up the daily routine of the rehearsals as they went

The first page of James's letter to Edmund Gosse upon hearing of Stevenson's death.

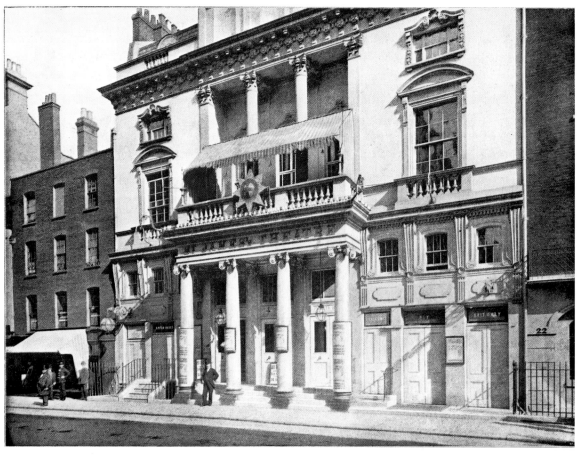

St James's Theatre, King Street, demolished in 1957.

George Alexander as Guy Domville.

A scene from Alexander's production of *Guy Domville*.

forward under Alexander's direction. That handsome and popular actor liked costume plays and felt that James's drama would give him not only a chance to display his physique in romantic-looking clothes, but also an opportunity to play the rewarding role of a young eighteenth-century aristocrat making an agonizing choice between the demands of an inherited estate and entrance into a Benedictine monastery. Alexander mounted the production superbly: electric lighting appeared for the first time at the St James's Theatre, outmoding gas-light. He expected much from this play, and James hoped desperately for success.

On the day *Guy Domville* was to open, two mysterious women dispatched a telegram to Alexander from the Sloane Street post office in Chelsea: WITH HEARTY WISHES FOR A COMPLETE FAILURE. Alexander didn't show this to the nervous author until after the performance. Rumour whispered around theatrical circles that one of the women was a disappointed actress whom Alexander had not given a job.

That evening, in an effort at distraction, James went to see Oscar Wilde's *An Ideal Husband* at the Haymarket Theatre, not far from the St James's. He was horrified as he sat among the chuckling audience and realized that this was what the public wanted. As he wrote to his brother William a few weeks later about the Wilde play,

The thing seemed to me so helpless, so crude, so bad, so clumsy, feeble and vulgar, that as I walked away across St James's Square to learn my own fate, the prosperity of what I had seen seemed to me to constitute a dreadful presumption of the shipwreck of G. D. [*Guy Domville*], and I stopped in the middle of the Square, paralysed by the terror of this probability – afraid to go on and learn more.

While Henry James had sat unhappily in the stalls over at the Haymarket, an impressive group had crowded into the St James's. It included the painters Sir Frederick Leighton, John Singer Sargent, and George Frederick Watts, as well as James's friends, the authors Mrs Humphry Ward and Edmund Gosse. George Bernard Shaw, already prominent as a writer on music and the theatre, was one of the drama critics present, along with the then little-known H. G. Wells and the almost totally unknown Arnold Bennett. There was a less distinguished crowd in the gallery, people who felt that 'Alick' would give them their money's worth. They included a rowdy element that didn't enjoy the play, and when George Alexander in the final act delivered the line, 'I'm the last, my lord, of the Domvilles', a voice from the gallery shouted, 'It's a bloody good thing y'are.'

The innocent author arrived at the stage door of the St James's a few minutes before the final curtain, and as he stepped back-stage he listened to the heavy applause from the stalls as the play ended. Alexander was receiving his customary ovation, though his drawn face projected disaster. Turning to the wings, he saw the author, for whom there had been cries, and he led the unsuspecting James out to the glaring new footlights. H. G. Wells later said that 'a spasm of hate for the writer' must have motivated Alexander, for

I have never heard any sound more devastating than the crescendo of booing that ensued. The gentle applause of the stalls was altogether overwhelmed. For a moment or so James faced the storm, his round face white above the beard, his mouth opening and shutting, and then Alexander, I hope in a contrite mood, snatched him back into the wings.

But when Edmund Gosse appeared early the next morning at 34 De Vere Gardens, he assumed that James had slept well; he was apparently enjoying his breakfast: 'The theatrical bubble in which he had lived a tormented existence for five years was wholly and finally broken, and he returned, even in that earliest conversation, to the discussion of the work he had so long and so sadly neglected, the art of direct prose narrative.'

Luncheon guests on that day, however, found a less confident James, a man fatigued after all the weeks of rehearsal and rewriting and being forced into the constant necessity to abbreviate – which James referred to as 'the foul fiend Excision!'

The leading critics, including William Archer and Clement Scott, reviewed *Guy Domville* favourably; Bernard Shaw in the *Saturday Review* was particularly friendly to the play. But it lasted only a month, bringing James royalties of £750. *Guy Domville* had been 'whisked away to make room for the triumphant Oscar' – referring to Wilde's *The Importance of Being Earnest*, which Alexander had hurried into production. That comedy proved to be abundantly successful,

(*Above*) Gertrude Elliott as Mrs Gracedew in *The High Bid*.

(*Above left*) The moment in Act III when Mrs Gracedew makes the High Bid: 'Now tell me, how much?'

and it was still on when catastrophe overtook Wilde, a matter in which James showed a lively interest, speaking of it as 'squalid' and 'tragic' and of having 'a sickening horribility'. At the St James's Theatre, George Alexander tried to keep *Earnest* going, even blotting out the author's name on the playbills; but despite its superiority to *An Ideal Husband*, attendance fell off, and Alexander had to close the play.

As for Henry James, he had little love left for the theatre despite the encouragement of some critics and managers. His play *The High Bid* in 1907 provided a starring role for the actress Gertrude Elliott, with her husband Johnston (later Sir Johnston) Forbes-Robertson in a secondary part. They staged it in Edinburgh and later in London, in the latter case only for special matinées. Audiences liked it, but it disappeared from the stage, perhaps because Forbes-Robertson was too engrossed in enjoying the success of his lifetime in Jerome K. Jerome's *The Passing of the Third Floor Back*.

On 14 February 1895, just after the failure of *Guy Domville*, James had a conversation with himself (through the medium of his note-book), at once involuted and profound, an exceptional example of a man working out a complex and aching problem at the very core where art and life meet; we can follow him step by step through this anguishing but, at the last, successful debate with himself:

I have my head, thank God, full of visions. One has never too many – one has never enough. Ah, just to let one's self go – at last: to surrender one's self to what through all the long years one has (quite ironically, I think) hoped for and waited for – the mere potential, and relative, increase of *quantity* in the material act – act of application and production. One has prayed and hoped and wanted, in a word, to be able to work *more*. And now, toward the end, it seems, within its limits, to have come. . . . Has a *part* of all this wasted passion and squandered time (of the last 5 years) been simply the precious lesson, taught me in that roundabout and devious, that cruelly expensive, way, *of the singular value for a narrative plan* too of the (I don't know *what* adequately to call it) divine principle of the Scenario? If that *has* been one side of the moral of the whole unspeakable, the whole tragic experience, I almost bless the pangs and the pains and the miseries of it. IF there has lurked in the central core of it this exquisite truth – I almost hold my breath with suspense as I try to formulate it; so much, so *much*, hangs radiantly there as depending on it – this exquisite truth that what I call the divine principle in question is a key that, working in the same *general* way fits the complicated chambers of *both* the narrative and the dramatic lock: IF, I say, I have crept round through long apparent barrenness, through suffering a sadness intoler-able to that rare perception – why my infinite little loss is converted into an almost infinite little gain. The [discovery] vivifies, backwardly – or appears to, a little – all the thankless faith, the unblessed work. But how much of the precious there may be in it, I can only tell by trying.

(*Opposite*) Henry James in 1894, by Philip Burne-Jones.

Part of the passage from the note-books, cited above.

In 1895, retreating from his over-burdened social life in London, James found some relief in the sea-side town of Torquay in Devonshire. 'I loved my Torquay to the end,' he said.

This is a document of vision and courage. After years of public neglect of his novels, and after the fiasco of his attempts to be successful in the theatre, James was a man gravely wounded and abysmally depressed. But in this self-discussion he shows that he can rise above agonies of disappointment. He was in his fifties: other men might simply have quit or have been worn out; but James faced his problems heroically. That entry in his notebook scrutinizes the most critical event in his life since he had first chosen to live in Europe twenty years earlier. Now he was ready to begin a new phase of his writing. This beginning was not easy; indeed, it was a long time before he got back to producing seriously. But the thing was there.

In the spring of 1895 he made another brief visit to Ireland, which he had been to in 1883 and 1891 and had not particularly liked, chiefly because of the squalor and bitterness of the Irish. Nor did he care much for the country on his third sojourn there. Invited to elaborate parties by high-ranking diplomats, he felt that the whole experience was 'a gorgeous bore', and he was again appalled by the miserable poverty he saw almost everywhere.

He returned to London in the summer, but found it was too much for him: 'The Americans looming up – dim, vast, portentous – in their millions – like gathering waves – the barbarians of the Roman Empire.' He sought refuge at Torquay, Devonshire, but even there his life was rather crowded. Nevertheless he worked away at a magazine serial called 'Old Things', later to be *The Spoils of Poynton*, and also wrote parts of *The Awkward Age*.

The idea for *The Spoils of Poynton* had come to him during a dinner-party, from a woman seated next to him at a 'table that glowed safe and fair through the brown London night'. The story he heard was of a mother and son who were fighting over the family furniture and other trappings that had been left to the son upon his father's death. This was the germ of the story for James, and he grieved at having to listen to the dinner-guest chattering on about the outcome of the situation, which showed 'clumsy Life again at her stupid work. . . . Life being all inclusion and confusion, and art being all discrimination and selection.' But James managed to preserve what he called the germ of the situation and to create his own tensely effective story around it.

On the steps of the Palazzo Borghese,
Rome, 1899.

The Spoils contains strong scenes, a sign that, as he had hoped, his theatrical experience was helping him to dramatize his narratives. *The Spoils* didn't appear as a book until 1897, and *The Awkward Age* not until 1899. That novel too showed the results of James's dramatic years, for the story is chiefly a matter of dialogue, beneath which James shrewdly investigates the effects upon a sensitive young girl of the worldly society of her time.

What Maisie Knew (1897) has a similar theme, involving an even younger girl; one might call her an old child. Forced from the age of six to begin dividing her time between her divorced parents, Maisie becomes increasingly aware of their lack of moral integrity. And as her elders remarry and continue to engage in infidelities, Maisie comes to know even more about such complications. Her knowledge of evil doesn't corrupt but rather strengthens her. She has to make a moral decision at the end of the story, which has a finely managed psychological twist. This novel again demonstrates James's concern with innocence and shows how greatly he admired victorious morality.

In 1896, before he had completed the serialized version of what was to become *The Spoils of Poynton*, James felt that he should live outside London. A friend found a temporary home for him at Playden, on the Sussex coast. James became fond of the area, with its picturesque old towns. His friend Kipling had said, on moving into Sussex, that he could feel history there twelve men deep. This is what James had always found in Europe, and now he discovered the kind of place he was looking for: English and ancient, and within easy reach of London.

When he had to move out of the house at Playden late in the summer because the owners were returning, he didn't want to go back to London and moved into the Old Vicarage at the near-by town of Rye. While there, he saw a fine old place he would like to live in: Lamb House. In 1897, when he received word that Lamb House was to be put up for rental, he at once made arrangements to live there. He eventually bought it, and it became his home for the rest of his life.

It is a remarkable house, built in the early eighteenth century, using parts of an older building. As James wrote to his brother William's wife,

I marked it for my own two years ago at Rye – so perfectly did it, the first instant I beheld it, offer the solution of my long-unassuaged desire for a calm retreat between May and November. It is the very calmest and yet cheerfullest that I could have dreamed – *in* the little old, cobble-stoned, grass-grown, red-roofed town, on the summit of its mildly pyramidal hill and close to its noble old church – the chimes of which will sound sweet in my goodly old red-walled garden.

The little place is so rural and tranquil, and yet discreetly animated, that its being within the town is, for convenience and immediate accessibility, purely to the good. ... I will try to have a photograph taken of the pleasant little old-world town-angle into which its nice old red-bricked front, its high old Georgian doorway and its

most delightful little old architectural garden-house, perched alongside of it on its high brick garden-wall – into which all these pleasant features together so happily 'compose'.

(*Above left*) Outside view of the studio at Lamb House, Rye.

(*Above*) The main entrance to Lamb House.

James was himself to compose in that garden-house in good weather. Long after his death, it was destroyed by a German bomb in the Second World War; but the rest of Lamb House has been preserved as it was in James's time.

Before moving there, he wrote one of the finest of his writers-and-artists stories, 'The Figure in the Carpet', serialized in 1896 and published in a collection of his tales later in that year, *Embarrassments*. 'The Figure in the Carpet' is a phrase used by the novelist in the story, Hugh Vereker, in suggesting what critics have always missed in his work. The young man to whom he says this sets out to find the secret pattern in Vereker's fiction, and James takes us through some intensive complications which, after Vereker's own demise, include the early deaths of the two people who know the answer to the riddle, but have not communicated it. This little fable for critics probably grew

An illustration by Philippe Jullian for 'The Turn of the Screw', 1946.

out of Henry James's feeling that his work was not really being under-stood, especially by his brother William, and he makes the story forcefully ironic.

Another tale he wrote before moving to Lamb House is the one for which he is best known, 'The Turn of the Screw'. This had its origin in a 'ghost-story' (as James called it in his notebook entry in 1895) told at a country-house party by the Archbishop of Canterbury. The notebook outline contains many of the elements James later used, such as children left in the care of servants who rather mysteriously die and then make dramatic reappearances. This last point has caused years of violent critical conflict between those who believe that the tale is indeed a ghost-story (James again called it that in the preface he wrote

Henry James in 1897, a drawing by William Rothenstein.

later) and those who assert that it is a psychological tale, the apparitions being hallucinated by the neurotic governess who is the narrator.

As James wrote in his notebook, 'It is all obscure and imperfect, the picture, the story, but there is a suggestion of strangely gruesome effect in it. The tale to be told – tolerably obviously – by an outside spectator, an observer.' But, after the reader's interest is kindled by a prologue chapter, the governess takes over the magnetic story. If her experience of seeing evil-looking apparitions at Bly were merely the extension of her own pathological imagination, as Edmund Wilson and several other critics have asserted, that would be horror enough, as the daemonic element itself would be, particularly since the two children are concerned; but if what the governess saw or thought she

James stood newly revealed when, at the turn of the century, he had his beard and moustache shaved off.

saw were at once pathological and diabolical, that would intensify the horror. The first time she 'sees' Peter Quint on the tower at sunset, she wonders whether there is 'a secret at Bly – a mystery of Udolpho or an insane, an unmentionable relative kept in unsuspected confinement' – this last suggests Rochester's secret in Charlotte Bronte's *Jane Eyre*, and the governess's own reference to Mrs Radcliffe's *The Mysteries of Udolpho* places the story unmistakably in the Gothic-novel tradition. The governess's further encounters or visions keep the narrative moving from one pitch of excitement to another, to the last outcry in the final paragraph. Whatever the author's motives – and exactly how evil or not evil were the children? – here is a master story-teller at his ripest.

In 1900, as if to meet the new century face to face, James had his beard and moustache shaved off, and a new personality emerged. The smooth face with the prominent profile, the near-baldness, made him look something like a Roman emperor on a coin. And his personality went more vigorously outward. Facial expressions which had long been pinched behind his beard now came into full view, and while he was often quiet in a social group, listening eagerly to all that was said, he was at times able to take over a conversation and master it. His

speech was slow, partly because he paused before carefully choosing his key words, and partly perhaps, as Mrs Wharton once suggested, because of the stammer he had when young.

James became a familiar figure in Rye. He frequently went on long walks or spun across the countryside on his bicycle, wearing golf clothes and a cap. Although he intensely disliked cats, he was often accompanied by a pet dog.

In the new century, James kept up many of his long-seasoned literary friendships, such as that with Edmund Gosse. Another of them was with the novelist Violet Hunt, whom he had first known when she was a young girl. But he was to turn away from her when she became Ford Madox Hueffer's mistress and the public target of his wife's shafts. In the course of time, however, James was willing to see Violet Hunt again.

He added various other men and women to his circle of acquaintances in the early years of the new century. Some of these, such as Joseph Conrad, lived not too far from Rye; Stephen Crane, who died in 1900, had also resided in the area, and James had several times visited him at his near-by manor, Brede Place. The young H. G. Wells was also a neighbour. But the fullest and longest lasting of the new

(*Above left*) Violet Hunt, the novelist and mistress of Ford Madox Hueffer. James called her his 'Purple Patch'.

(*Above right*) Max Beerbohm's 'memory of Henry James and Joseph Conrad conversing at an afternoon party, circa 1904'.

85

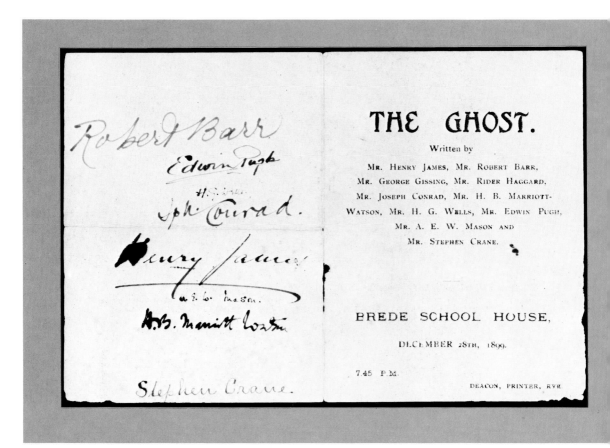

THE GHOST.

Written by

MR. HENRY JAMES, MR. ROBERT BARR,
MR. GEORGE GISSING, MR. RIDER HAGGARD,
MR. JOSEPH CONRAD, MR. H. B. MARRIOTT-
WATSON, MR. H. G. WELLS, MR. EDWIN PUGH,
MR. A. E. W. MASON AND
MR. STEPHEN CRANE.

BREDE SCHOOL HOUSE.

DECEMBER 28TH, 1899.

7.45 P.M.

DEACON, PRINTER, RYE.

The autographed programme of a play presented during a large Christmas-week party organized by the Stephen Cranes at Brede Place to welcome the year 1900. The party terminated with the onset of Crane's fatal illness.

friendships was that with Edith Wharton, who usually set up her headquarters in France. Her husband Edward (Teddy) Wharton was in and out of mental homes, and her emotional life had found a focus in Walter Berry, an American lawyer in Paris. Mrs Wharton admired James's work almost to the point of discipleship. They had met earlier socially but James had paid little attention to her although she dressed brilliantly for the encounters. After he had read some of her fiction, however, he welcomed her as a friend. She was among the early owners of an automobile and James often went on motor tours with her, in her chauffeur-driven car, in both England and France. James found her delightful, with a kind of humour they could share, but she often intruded on his work, taking up hours or days he wanted to devote to his writing. He made up an amusing series of names for her; the one he used most often was Angel of Devastation.

The years 1899–1900 were extremely productive, for at that time James wrote an astounding number of short stories, as well as prose pieces of other kinds. In 1900, after returning from a trip to Italy, he embarked on *The Sacred Fount*, intending to keep it to ten thousand

Henry James and Cora, the
common-law wife of Stephen Crane,
during a party at Brede Place in
August 1899.

James, Edith Wharton, and Edward
Wharton (beside the chauffeur) on
tour in France in 'the chariot of fire'.

The climactic final moment in James's novella 'The Beast in the Jungle', a lithograph by Charles Demuth, *c.* 1924.

words. But as he went on elaborating this story of various mysterious relationships at a country-estate party, it became a novel of some seventy thousand words, which both breaks away from his past and presages his future. It is one of the most elaborately puzzling of his novels, even more so than *What Maisie Knew* and *The Awkward Age*, and it forms a distinct path to the complex and yet less mystifying novels of the next few years: *The Wings of the Dove* (1902), *The Ambassadors* (1903), and *The Golden Bowl* (1904), which bring James's writing to its zenith.

One of the remarkable novellas he wrote during these years is 'The Beast in the Jungle', in which a man meets a woman in Naples and tells her of his premonition of his destiny. As she recalls it when they meet again in England eight years later:

You said you had from your earliest time, as the deepest thing within you, the sense of being kept for something rare and strange, possibly prodigious and terrible, that was sooner or later to happen to you, that you had in your bones the foreboding and the conviction of, and that would perhaps overwhelm you.

Across the years that follow, the man and woman see one another frequently, but in his self-absorption he fails to perceive her feeling for him. She tells him that she has understood his secret, but it is not revealed until the last climactic scene, after her death, when he visits her grave and in a moment of shocked recognition at last understands his terrible doom.

Of the long novels of this last period, *The Ambassadors* was completed before *The Wings of the Dove* but, because the former book was scheduled to be serialized, it was held back for book publication until 1903. It marks the first aspect of what F. O. Matthiessen, followed by numerous other critics, called James's 'major phase'.

James found *The Ambassadors* more formally satisfying than his earlier work. It grew out of an entry in his notebook dated 1895: the record of a young friend's meeting with William Dean Howells in Whistler's garden in Paris. Howells had told him to grasp all he could of youth, for youth was the great thing: 'I'm old. It's too late. It has gone past me – I've lost it. You have time. You are young. Live!'

William Dean Howells.

James's novel is partly lyrical, a hymn to the wonder of Paris as it gradually invades the consciousness of Strether, the aging protagonist, at the same time planting in him new sets of values. At length a sentence similar to that of Howells is wrung from him, as he addresses a young American abroad. By taking Strether's mind as the chief scene of the novel's drama, and by seeing the events through his eyes, James was able to establish a keenly reflective story-centre; indeed, the reader not only sees the complicated plot from the inside, but he also participates in Strether's response and gradual surrender to the attraction of Paris.

The spell of Europe begins to make itself felt early in the story when Strether, soon after landing at Liverpool, goes out to see the medieval wall around near-by Chester, as he had done thirty years before, as a young man. James provides, through Strether's consciousness, a remarkable sentence which illustrates the Jamesian 'law of successive

Place de l'Opéra, Paris; a painting of 1901.

Jean Béraud
1901

An American cartoonist's response to the entanglements of James's late prose style.

Aspects' (an idea developed in relation to story plots). There are few sentences in James or any other writer which so masterfully take the reader along, presenting all the ups and downs of the setting, the points at which the vision is caught and those at which it hurries on:

The tortuous wall – girdle long since snapped, of the little swollen city, half held in place by careful civic hands – wanders in narrow file between parapets smoothed by peaceful generations, pausing here and there for a dismantled gate or bridged gap, with rises and drops, steps up and steps down, queer twists, queer contacts, peeps into homely streets and under the brows of gables, views of cathedral tower and waterside fields, of huddled English town and ordered English country.

This is not mere decoration: it is an augury of the plot of the novel, suggesting its circular nature, full of elaborate twists, but ultimately observing a pattern of order.

The Wings of the Dove takes place in London and Venice, and in the atmosphere of the latter James again makes scenery an aspect of the plot, which in the main concerns itself with the scheme hatched by Kate Croy, in love with the impecunious journalist Merton Densher. Her strategy is to induce Merton to marry the heiress Milly Theale, who is mortally ill; after her death, Merton would have enough money to marry Kate. Milly, the bright and attractive American girl, is another of James's fictional portraits of Minny Temple.

The Wings of the Dove begins with an unusual style of phrasing: 'She waited, Kate Croy, for her father to come in . . .' and then the sentence goes on, to moderate length. Why this odd sentence? Why not, simply, 'Kate Croy waited for her father to come in . . .' – and so forth, as any other novelist would have written? Some commentators might suggest that James's beginning for that sentence came out of his dictating his work, a method he had adopted since writing now caused his right wrist to ache. But there is something more than the merely stenographic in this opening clause with its appositional commas: James was presenting people who dealt in indirection, beginning with Kate and her father. That opening strikes a note of deviousness, hinting at the twisting and crooked progress of Kate's plot, though it is Milly herself who dominates the story and, even in death, defeats Kate – as James shows in the last scene, even in the last line of the story.

If the American girl ultimately wins in the subtle yet desperate conflict in *The Wings of the Dove*, another of her species does so more decisively – and lives through her victory – in *The Golden Bowl*. This too is a tortuous story with frequent dramatic heightening of the action. Maggie, a rich American girl in London, marries the Italian Prince Amerigo, but retains her urgent closeness to her father, as in the similar case of Clover Hooper Adams. In *The Golden Bowl*, the neglected Prince resumes an adulterous affair with Charlotte, a friend of Maggie's.

Maggie, who knows nothing of their past relations, accidentally becomes aware of the liaison between Amerigo and Charlotte, and the medium of her realization is the symbolic golden bowl of the title. She thinks of a grand revenge one night as she paces the terrace of her father's countryhouse. In one of the most magnificent scenes in all modern literature, she strides back and forth, seeing most of the principal characters in the story playing bridge in a bright room. She knows what she can do to launch her revenge, how she could cry out greatly against her wrong:

Spacious and splendid, like a stage awaiting a drama, it was a scene she might people, by the press of her spring, either with serenities and decencies and dignities, or with terrors and shames and ruins, things as ugly as those formless fragments of her golden bowl she was trying so hard to pick up.

Out in the darkness, seeing the cardplayers, she has an intense vision of her wrong, and in her consciousness the possibility of vengeance turns itself aside:

Bronzino's painting of Lucrezia Panciatichi has been suggested as the portrait mentioned in *The Wings of the Dove* for its resemblance to Milly Theale.

In the garden at Lamb House, 1901.

She might fairly, as she watched them, have missed it as a lost thing; have yearned for it, for the straight vindictive view, the rights of resentment, the rage of jealousy, the protests of passion, as for something she had been cheated of not least; a range of feeling which for many women would have meant so much, but which for *her* husband's wife, for *her* father's daughter, figured nothing nearer to experience than a wild eastern caravan, looming into view with crude colours in sun, fierce pipes in the air, high spears against the sky, all a thrill, a natural joy to mingle with, but turning short before it reached her and plunging into other defiles.

Here is a supreme example at the high moment of a story, of the use of metaphor-symbol, with that vividly impressive caravan turning away, as Maggie ('*her* husband's wife, *her* father's daughter') puts aside her temptation.

One of the principal achievements of this novel is its portrayal of the delicate feelings of people who, even in committing a wrong, don't wish to hurt anyone else. At the end, when Amerigo and Maggie are together again, with their small son, they are together for good. But they are aware that life can be grim, for as the Prince tells Maggie, 'Everything's terrible, *cara*, in the heart of man.'

In 1897 James had hired a young secretary, a Scotsman named William MacAlpine. Because of MacAlpine's ability to take short-hand, and because James preferred direct use of the typewriter, the secretary's talents were being wasted, and James found another job for him in 1901. He then engaged a young woman, Mary Weld.

94

On a walk through the grounds of Lamb House with Mrs Humphry Ward.

During James's long pauses in dictation, while his mind circum-navigated the sentences to their usually forceful conclusions, MacAlpine had smoked. Miss Weld crocheted. In 1904, during James's absence in America, however, she married, so upon his return he engaged Theodora Bosanquet, a well-educated young woman with literary interests who, during the pauses in dictation, would read a book. Miss Bosanquet remained with James for the last eleven years of his life.

He was not a wealthy man; his inheritance had been small, and he lived entirely by his writing; he lived expensively, and since he was not a popular author like his friends Mrs Humphry Ward and Edith Wharton, he had to work hard and continuously at his writing. He travelled in *de luxe* style, and he kept a domestic staff at Lamb House,

(*Above left*) Theodora Bosanquet, the last of James's three secretaries, who remained with him for the final eleven years of his life.

(*Above right*) Burgess Noakes.

which was first presided over by a couple named Smith, the man as butler-valet, the woman as cook. The Smiths had been with James since 1886, when he had first gone to live at 34 De Vere Gardens. Their increasing addiction to alcohol was never really intrusive at the London flat, but it became worse at Lamb House, and once in 1901 they became so drunk that James ordered them out, in what he later referred to as a 'domestic cyclone'. He also had at Lamb House a gardener, a cook-housekeeper, a parlour-maid, a housemaid, and a local boy, Burgess Noakes, eventually to become bantamweight champion of Sussex and James's valet and butler, whom his employer called 'my gnome Burgess'. James had given up his flat in De Vere Gardens, but usually avoided the winters at Rye by staying in London at the Reform Club, one of several he belonged to. He furnished his own quarters at the Reform and kept them on a permanent basis, to use when he came up from Rye.

A corner of the Athenaeum Club, Pall Mall, one of James's headquarters in London.

The Reform Club, where James usually stayed on his winter visits from Rye.

97

Another view – this one by Beer-bohm – of James's style and his ambiguous relations with America.

In August 1904, after two decades of absence, he revisited the United States. He even went to California and Florida for the first time. But he spent most of his year on the Eastern Seaboard he used to know so well. The new aspect of New York both fascinated and repelled him; he found in its 'note of vehemence . . . a particular type of dauntless power' which had a special kind of appeal. One of his melancholy moments was a visit to the site of his 'ruthlessly suppressed birth-house' which had once stood in Washington Place.

That was where the pretense that nearly nothing was changed had most to come in; for a high, square, impersonal structure, proclaiming its lack of interest with a crudity all its own, so blocks, at the right moment for its own success, the view of the past, that the effect for me, in Washington Place, was of having been amputated of half its history. . . .

– an observation that will touch many of his fellow countrymen; this is a cardinal statement by America's most notable *déraciné*.

In New England, usually visiting friends, he discovered, particularly in the autumnal colours, that much of the country's natural beauty was intact. He went to Edith Wharton's estate at Lennox, Massachusetts, as well as to his brother William's residence in Cambridge (95 Irving Street) and his summer home at Chocorua, New Hampshire. Henry in recent years had seen William on his trips abroad, sometimes with his wife and children. Yet while Henry was in America, unexpectedly becoming a figure in the public Press – even the target of cartoonists – William James went abruptly to Greece, to which he had never been before. After his return he found that he had been elected to the American Academy of Arts and Letters, two months after his brother Henry was chosen. In June 1905 William wrote to the Academy refusing to accept its election. One reason he gave was

The home of William James in Cambridge, Massachusetts.

that perhaps the James influence would be too strong. He also said, amazingly, 'I am the more encouraged in this course by the fact that my younger and shallower and vainer brother is already in the Academy.'

The controversy over this statement has not ended to this day. In the columns of the *Times Literary Supplement* as recently as 1972, it was defended by some as no more than a family jest, while others considered it in the light of Freudian psychology as an expression, however teasing, of the unconscious animosity in William's feelings about his brother. Though the latter interpretation has support else-where in the James family papers, not every reader will agree that William's most private feelings could have vented themselves publicly in so transparent a fashion.

Henry's American trip included lectures in different parts of the country, to social clubs or to university audiences, and these platform appearances paid for his year's travels. He was an unexpectedly forceful lecturer, usually speaking on Balzac, 'for whom', as he told his listeners, 'I entertain a great esteem'. James, upon his return to England, wrote the travel essays which were to make up his book *The American Scene* (1907). In this he dealt with the East Coast, including Florida; he hoped to write another volume concerned with his first visits to California and the Middle West, but he never did so.

Back at Lamb House he had many literary visitors, among them the young artists and writers who regarded him as the Master. There was also a young Irishman who was not a writer, Dudley Jocelyn Persse, the nephew of Lady Gregory of the Irish Renaissance. No one seemed to stand closer in James's affections, which were reciprocated and lasted from 1903 to James's last illness. Another strong friendship involved the Norwegian-born, Boston-reared sculptor, Hendrik Christian Andersen, who had a studio in Rome on the Via Margutta. They first met in 1899, when James had bought from Andersen the bust of a youthful Italian nobleman which he sent on to Rye. The tall, handsome, blond Andersen visited Lamb House, and James (who had seen him again in America) went to Rome, for his last time, in 1907, after Andersen had gone back there in the wake of several artistic failures in New York. Andersen now moved to the Villa Helena, near the Piazza del Popolo, and invited James to stay with him there, but James preferred a place he had stopped at before, the Hôtel de Russie, on the Via del Babuino, just off the south-east edge of the Piazza. The building, formerly the Russian Embassy, later to become the headquarters of Radio Italiana, has a charming garden on the lower slope of the Pincian Hill, as well as fountains and birds and antique statues. But James no longer loved Rome as in the past: 'The abatements and changes and modernisms and vulgarities,' he wrote to William's son Billy, 'the crowd and the struggle and the frustration

The two brothers, Henry and William James.

Henry James in New York, 1906.

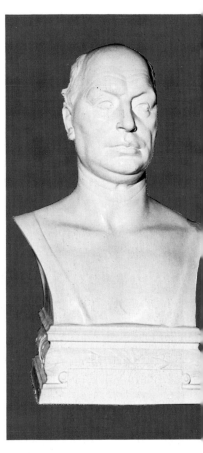

(*Above*) On his last visit to Italy, in 1907, James paused to visit friends at Vallombrosa, 'a dream of Tuscan loveliness'. Seated, from left, Howard Sturgis, Mrs and Mr Edward Boit.

(*Above right*) The bust of James executed by Hendrik Andersen in 1907.

(of real communion with what one wanted) are quite dreadful'; he could 'quite revel in the thought that I shall never come to Italy *at all* again'.

James enjoyed seeing Hendrik Andersen in Rome, and he sat for a bust of himself that looks rather coldly gross. But he was apparently alarmed by the sculptures in Andersen's studio, enormous men and women trying to look ecstatic but succeeding for the most part in appearing only frantic. When, a few years later, Andersen began planning an immense world city, with a Tower of Progress and a Temple of the Arts, and his own gigantic statues in all the green places, James could no longer conceal his alarm at the grandiosity of the friend to whom he had once addressed a letter, 'Dearest, dearest, more tenderly embraced than I can say!' In 1912, James sent Andersen a warning about his 'mania for the colossal':

I have practically said all these things to you before – though perhaps never in so dreadfully straight and sore a form as today, when this culmination of your madness, to the tune of five hundred millions of tons of weight, simply squeezes it out of me. For that, dearest boy, is the Dread Delusion to warn you against – what is called in

Medical Science MEGALOMANIA (look it up in the dictionary!) in French *la folie des grandeurs*, the infatuated and disproportionate love and pursuit of, and attempt at, the Big, the Bigger, the Biggest, the Immensest Immensity, with all sense for proportion, application, relation and possibility madly submerged.

The correspondence continued, with James remaining fairly cool. He and Andersen met for the last time when the sculptor stopped off in England in 1915, on his way to America. Andersen returned to Rome after the war, became a friend of King Victor Emmanuel II, and died there in 1939, when he was sixty-seven. He willed all his statues and his plans for the vast metropolis to the Commune of Rome, and they may still be seen in his studio on the ground floor of the Villa Helena, which with the passing of time became a lodging-house.

A few of the heroic figures in Hendrik Andersen's studio in Rome.

Hugh Walpole as a young man.

Other relationships with young men were to prove less strenuous. In 1909 Henry James met Hugh Walpole, already a mediocre novelist but not yet knighted. James wrote warmly affectionate letters to Lawrence also. A different type of young writer closely associated with James, apparently without receiving one of his affectionate 'dearest boy' notes, was H. G. Wells, who in the early part of the twentieth century built an enormous reputation, not only with his science fiction, but also with his novels in the mode of Dickens. His book *Marriage* (1912) was the subject of a lively discussion with James, which Wells reported in his *Experiment in Autobiography* (1934). In the novel two young people drove their donkey-carts into a side lane and remained there talking for three hours. The author didn't present their

H.G. Wells about the time James first met him.

conversation, but merely commented that, by the time they left, they were engaged. James was quite vigorous about what he considered the wrongness of this: the novelist should focus on such a significant scene, projecting its particulars and the conversation of the two young people, as well as dramatizing the psychology of the situation. Wells said such things didn't matter. He just wanted to get on with the story. James's criticism of Wells's methods came out into the open in his two articles on 'The Younger Generation' in the *Times Literary Supplement* in 1914. He repeated there his criticism of Wells and other realists such as Arnold Bennett, who 'let affirmation of energy, however directed or undirected, constitute for them the "treatment" of the theme'. In the following year, Wells showed his irritation at James in the book *Boon* (with its triple subtitle, *The Mind of the Race*, *The Wild Asses of the Devil* and *The Last Trump*). James could accept parody and chuckled over his friend Max Beerbohm's 'The Mote in the Middle Distance', as he would probably have chortled, many years later, at James Thurber's 'The Beast in the Dingle' – both Beerbohm and Thurber were staunch admirers of James, and their pieces were light and amusing without being malicious. But Wells's discussion and lampoon of James in *Boon* were bitter and offensive. James wrote a dignified letter of protest, and Wells answered with a half-apology which James didn't accept. In the last of all his letters to Wells, James speaks out of injury but with great dignity. The letter ends:

It is art that *makes* life, makes interest, makes importance, for our consideration and applications of these things, and I know of no substitute whatever for the force and beauty of its process. If I were Boon I should say that any pretense of such a sub-stitute is helpless and hopeless humbug; but I wouldn't be Boon for the world, and am only yours faithfully

Henry James

James needed comfort in those years; he had suffered a number of disappointments. One of them was the failure of the collected 'New York Edition' of his writings, which came out in twenty-four volumes, as *The Novels and Tales of Henry James*, between 1907 and 1909. It took him nearly three years (1906–8) to revise the texts of the novels and stories he had selected, and to write the informative prefaces to them which appeared separately as *The Art of the Novel* (edited by R.P. Blackmur) in 1934.

In 1908 James learned from Charles Scribner's Sons, his publishers, that his first royalties on the already issued volumes of the 'New York Edition' were only $211. Angst overtook him; he had thought that the collected volumes would keep him fairly well-to-do in his old age. Now at sixty-five he suffered a nervous depression far more serious than the one at the time of *Guy Domville*. Then he had plunged at once into work and his crisis passed. But now he felt he couldn't write. He consulted a heart specialist and even the noted physician, Sir William Osler, and both doctors reassured him. Yet what he called his 'black depression' lingered.

William James and his wife Alice crossed the Atlantic to see Henry and try to cheer him. They travelled on the Continent, where William, plagued by heart trouble, once again visited his favourite spa, Bad Nauheim. While they were in Zürich, word came that Robertson James had died of a heart attack; Henry and Alice kept the news from William for a while.

Henry, with his valet Burgess Noakes, returned to America with his brother and sister-in-law. They went to New Hampshire, and there at his summer home, William, who had been in great pain and discomfort, died on 26 August 1910. After the funeral in a chapel at Harvard, Henry James stayed on in America for nearly a year, mostly at William's house in Cambridge. He tried to keep out of public notice, and often went down to New York, where he consulted various doctors, including one who was familiar with the new Freudian theories.

Harvard gave Henry James an honorary degree in the spring of 1911, which he accepted 'with deference to William's memory – though he was so infinitely more to Harvard than Harvard ever was to, or for, him'. William was much on his mind when, after his return to England and Lamb House in 1911, Henry found himself able once more to resume his writing. He began his autobiographical series, *A Small Boy and Others* (1913), *Notes of a Son and Brother* (1914), and the unfinished third volume, *The Middle Years*, published in 1917, after his death. These are all notable for their portraits of his father and William, as well as for their revelation of many of Henry's important experiences.

In 1911 the last of his novels to be published in James's lifetime also appeared. A prose-fiction version of one of his earlier plays, *The Outcry* is decidedly weak in comparison with the three novels he had brought out in the first years of the century.

During these years James made a remarkable and unexpected public appearance at a performance of *Oedipus the King*, staged by Max Reinhardt at Covent Garden in 1912 with John Martin-Harvey in the title-role. Reinhardt wanted to make the audience part of the action: the chorus marched through the pit and mounted two staircases to the stage. One evening during this procession a latecomer was accidentally caught up by the actors, and when the chorus arrived on stage and parted, they revealed a baldheaded man in evening clothes, the bewildered Henry James.

A scene from Max Reinhardt's production of *Oedipus the King*.

James could be theatrically spectacular. Hugh Walpole remembered walking with him through fields near Rye, until they came to a gate that two grimy urchins opened. James reached in his pocket for some pennies, and began a solemn lecture about sweet-shops in the town, particularly one where they were to go with these pennies and purchase a certain kind of sweet: was it called 'Honey-nut', or 'Rye's Delight', or perhaps 'Honey Delight', or could it be – but at this point the children turned away in terror and ran screaming across the fields. James looked in bewilderment at the coppers in his hand, wondering what could have possibly made the children run off. He had meant only kindness. The episode left him disturbed for days.

Edith Wharton recalled an occasion on which she and James were in her car on a rainy evening going into Windsor, where her chauffeur's understudy couldn't find the King's Road. James in the back seat undertook to locate the proper direction, and as the car stopped beside an old man who had been staring at it, James leaned out and said, 'My good man, if you'll be good enough to come here, please; a little nearer, so.' The old man moved closer, and James proceeded:

My friend, to put it to you in two words, this lady and I have just arrived here from Slough; that is to say, to be more strictly accurate, have recently *passed through* Slough on our way here, having actually motored to Windsor from Rye, which was our point of departure; and the darkness having overtaken us, we should be much obliged if you would tell us where we are now in relation to the High Street, which, as you of course know, leads to the Castle, after leaving on the left hand the turn down to the railway station.

He went on, 'In short' – which Mrs Wharton noted would begin more 'explanatory ramifications' –

in short, my good man, what I want to put to you in a word is this: supposing we have already (as I have reason to think we have) driven past the turn down to the railroad station (which in that case, by the way, would probably not have been on our left hand, but on our right), where are we now in relation to . . .

At this, Mrs Wharton said, 'Oh, please, do ask him where the King's Road is.'

'Ah – ? The King's Road? Just so! Quite right! Can you, as a matter of fact, my good man, tell us where, in relation to our present position, the King's Road exactly *is*?'

The old man said, 'Ye're in it.'

In other circumstances, Mrs Wharton says, James's involutions were greatly appreciated by his friends for their subtleties or their often hidden wit. In the last phase of his career, he wrote as he talked, complicatedly but effectively.

He left behind two unfinished novels, both published in 1917: *The Ivory Tower* and *The Sense of the Past*. The former is set in the Newport

H. O. Nicholson and Leslie Howard in *Berkeley Square*, the play adapted from James's unfinished novel, *The Sense of the Past*.

James had known so long ago, and deals with the effects of great wealth upon various men and women. In *The Sense of the Past*, a young American who has inherited a house in London suddenly steps into the past, and finds himself living among men and women of the 1820s. This story, completed and adapted for the stage as *Berkeley Square*, by John Balderston, was a theatrical success in the late 1920s. The action of the play was moved back from the 1820s to the age of Dr Johnson. *The Sense of the Past* is in some ways reminiscent of James's tale of 1908, 'The Jolly Corner'. In this *Dorian Gray*-like story an American who has spent most of his life in Europe returns at

fifty-six to see an old house he has inherited which is near 'a jolly corner' in downtown New York. He has often wondered what he would be like if he had remained in America, and one night in the house he is confronted by a figure in evening clothes whose face bears some resemblance to his own but is hideous and loathsome.

James, the man who had stayed on in Europe, was in the years just before the First World War in poor financial condition. Because of this, Edith Wharton secretly arranged with her American publishers (who were also James's), the house of Scribner, to turn over $8,000 of her royalties to him, under the pretence that it was an advance on future work. She also tried ardently, again without James's knowledge, to obtain the Nobel Prize for him, but she failed to do so. Mrs Wharton, however, was not going to be stopped: in the winter of 1912–13, she wrote to various Americans to try to raise a fund in honour of Henry James on his seventieth birthday, 15 April 1913. He heard of Mrs Wharton's actions through his nephew Billy, and cabled him to have all the money which had so far been given turned back to the donors. The birthday was celebrated, however, by a subscription taken up among various friends of James's in England. They also arranged to have John Singer Sargent, who had sketched him in the past, paint his portrait for the occasion.

The picture, now in the National Portrait Gallery, was in 1913 on exhibition at the Royal Academy. One day a feminist, Mrs May Wood, visited the Academy, wearing a cloak that concealed a meat-cleaver. She stalked up to the portrait, broke the glass protecting it, and began hacking away at the figure of James – a man sympathetic to the 'women's-rights' cause. The frantic feminist managed to make three gashes in the painting before she was snatched away. At the police station she announced that she was calling attention to the neglect of women: no woman painter would have received Sargent's reported fee of £700. James said in a letter to a friend that he naturally felt 'quite scalped and disfigured'; but the painting could be repaired.

Earlier in that year, James had given up his quarters at the Reform Club, principally because he couldn't bring in a woman typist. In January he moved to a large flat at 21 Carlyle Mansions, Chelsea, which had a striking view of the Thames. Miss Bosanquet, who lived not far away, continued as his typist; and there were separate rooms for a cook and a maid and the now indispensable valet, Burgess Noakes.

After the war broke out – and Noakes had to join the army – James, now suddenly an 'alien', noted how difficult it was for him to get about, particularly in going down to Lamb House. Because it was in a coastal zone, he continually had to obtain special permission to travel in that area, and once there he had to report regularly to the police. But these nuisances were only part of the reason why he decided to

(*Opposite*) Henry James at seventy, by John Singer Sargent.

In 1913 James left his rooms at the Reform Club and moved into his final home, a flat at 21 Carlyle Mansions, Cheyne Walk, Chelsea, with a wide view over the Thames.

A portion of the waterfront at Rye.

A portrait of Gosse by Sargent.

James's note to Edmund Gosse, containing a copy of his formal statement of application for British citizenship.

become a British subject: he was irritated that the United States hadn't at once rallied to the Anglo-French cause to help save civilization from the Germans. In 1915, his friend Gosse helped him obtain British citizenship; the Prime Minister, H.H. Asquith, gladly became one of the signatories of his application. On 28 July Henry James took his oath of allegiance to King George V and happily announced, 'Civus Britannicus sum', and then rather thoughtfully said that he felt no whit 'different'.

His friendship with Herbert Asquith and his wife, the volatile Margot, led to an amusing encounter at their Castle, Walmer, on the Kentish coast. James was a week-end guest, along with Winston Churchill, then the youthful and brilliant First Lord of the Admiralty. Churchill, accustomed to an easy dominance over dinner-table con-

Winston Churchill in 1915.
Meeting Churchill, James said,
'brought home to me very forcibly –
very vividly – the *limitations* by which
men of genius obtain their ascendancy . . .'.

versations, was disgruntled when he discovered that James's talk was receiving everyone's full attention as he went on and on. Churchill's attempts at interruption were ridden down by James, as he continued to utter his circuitous sentences which had pauses that somehow Churchill couldn't break into as James searched for the correctly emphatic words to intensify his phrases. James later dropped a kindly reference to the baffled Churchill, quietly telling Herbert Asquith's daughter Violet (Lady Bonham Carter) that it had been a very interesting, 'very encouraging experience to meet that young man. It brought home to me very forcibly – very vividly – the *limitations* by which men of genius obtain their ascendancy over mankind.' Falling somewhat into Churchill's manner, James concluded, 'It bucks one up.'

It was unusual, in any event, for James to be put down conversationally. But Percy Lubbock, who in 1920 edited James's letters, recalled a time when the novelist could make no conversational headway against the assaults of his dear friend the Welsh-born novelist Rhoda Broughton, whom he liked in spite of her violent approach to discussions, her slapdash manner which made genuine talk, with its give and take, difficult if not impossible.

At one country week-end party James, sitting with formidable massiveness among the guests, began a discourse on Shakespeare, wondering how such great creations could have come from the Stratford 'lout' – at which word, Rhoda Broughton burst forth, 'A lout! me divine William a lout?'

'But wait, dear lady, wait – see where I'm coming out – he reappears, as I say, this lout from Stratford –'

But the woman novelist cried out again that she would not have her divine William called a lout. James, heavily trying to maintain control, went on, 'In short, this lout –' and again was cut off: 'Me beloved Jamie calling Shakespeare a *lout*' – and she burst into laughter, destroying the conversation altogether.

James still dined out and went to country-house parties after the outbreak of war, but he severely reduced his social life and writing activities. He gave himself unstintingly to helping those who had suffered the miseries of war. He worked first with the Belgian Relief and made many hospital visits to wounded Belgian soldiers, a fitting assignment for him because his own use of French was so excellent. Eventually the circle of his service widened, and he became a familiar figure in military hospitals. Burgess Noakes, wounded and deafened by an exploding shell, returned to become valet-butler again at 21 Carlyle Mansions.

When James had time, he wrote essays about the war. After his death, a collection of them was published in a volume, *Within the Rim* (1918); a glance at some of the essay titles will give an idea of the book. Besides the one which provided the volume with its name, there are:

'Refugees in Chelsea', 'The American Volunteer Motor-Ambulance Corps in France', 'France' (a paean of praise for that country's culture and courage), and 'The Long Wards'.

War-time destruction, such as this at the Grande Place, Ypres, moved James deeply, and he gave generously of his time and energy in aid of the Belgian wounded.

On 2 December 1915, Henry James suffered a stroke in his flat at Carlyle Mansions and was carried to bed. He is reported as saying, 'So it has come at last – the Distinguished Thing.' Another stroke followed, and his mind drifted. As the days passed, he was sometimes lucid, sometimes incoherent. Occasionally Theodora Bosanquet continued her secretarial duties. In feverish interludes, James would dictate letters to members of Napoleon Bonaparte's family, insisting that these communications be signed 'Napoleone', in the Corsican style.

The literarily inclined Edward Marsh, former secretary to Winston Churchill and now on the staff of the Prime Minister, suggested that James be given the Order of Merit. Lord Morley, for whom James had long ago written his book on Hawthorne when as plain John Morley he was editing the English Men of Letters series, vigorously opposed the award. But Marsh won; Asquith took the matter to George V, who approved the O.M. for James. This was announced on New Year's Day, and the noted historian Lord Bryce brought the certificate to

James's bedside. After Bryce had left, the now fully conscious author told the housemaid to 'Turn off the light so as to spare my blushes.'

In the days that followed, his mind again became unstable, but he lived on until the evening of 28 February 1916. There was talk of burial in Westminster Abbey, but the Dean received the suggestion without enthusiasm and pointed out that the cost would be £100. Mrs William James and her daughter Peggy, who had crossed the Atlantic again, then arranged for the funeral to be held in Chelsea Old Church, where a memorial plaque now hangs on one of the walls. The day of the funeral was one of heavy rain, but many notables attended: Kipling, Sargent, Gosse and Ellen Terry were among the friends and admirers who crowded the church.

As he had wished, Henry James was cremated, and his ashes were taken back to America, to be put among the family graves in the cemetery at Cambridge. His reputation as a writer, not really high at the time, was virtually buried with his ashes. Those occupied with the spinning 1920s and the grim 1930s paid him little heed; but after a second war split the world apart, more people began to appreciate the intricacy and depth of James's writings, and such prescience as Prince Amerigo manifested in *The Golden Bowl*, when he said, 'Everything's terrible, *cara*, in the heart of man.' An eventual realization of the power of James's vision, of his sense of the complications of modern life, and of the psychological intensity of his stories has at last brought him to eminence.

James memorial tablet in Chelsea Old Church.

1843 Henry, second son of Henry and Mary James, born on 15 April at 21 Washington Place, New York City. A first son, William, had been born the previous year.

1843–45 Family visits Europe, staying in France and England.

1845–47 Family resides in Albany, N.Y.

1845 Birth of third son, Garth Wilkinson ('Wilky').

1846 Birth of fourth son, Robertson.

1847–55 Family resides in New York City. A daughter, Alice, born in 1848.

1855–58 Family travels in England, France, and Switzerland.

1858 Back in America, the family resides in Newport, Rhode Island.

1859 Family again in Europe. Henry attends schools in Geneva and Bonn.

1860 Family returns to Newport. Henry, with his brother William, studies art, also writes poems, and translates French authors.

1861 Henry injured while helping to put out a fire ('a horrid even if obscure hurt'). Wilky and Robertson fight on the Union side in the Civil War. William attends Lawrence Scientific School at Harvard.

1862–63 Henry spends year at Harvard Law School.

1864 Family leaves Newport for Boston. William goes to Harvard Medical School. Henry's first published story appears anonymously in the *Continental Monthly*.

1865 'The Story of a Year' appears under his own name, and marks the début of Henry James in the *Atlantic Monthly*.

1866–68 Family moves to Cambridge, Mass. Henry lives at home, continues his writing, begins friendship with William Dean Howells.

1869–70 Henry goes to Europe, travels in England, France, Switzerland, and Italy. In 1870 learns of the death of his cousin Minny Temple. Returns to America in the Spring.

1871 *Watch and Ward*, his first novel, serialized in the *Atlantic Monthly*.

1872–74 Henry again in Europe, writes travel articles. Frequent visits with William, now an instructor at Harvard, in Europe for his health.

1874–75 Continuing his writing career, Henry spends the winter in New York City, works on *Roderick Hudson*. His first two books published: *A Passionate Pilgrim and Other Tales* and *Transatlantic Sketches*. Realizing that he can make his living as a writer, he settles in Paris as correspondent for the *New York Tribune*. *Roderick Hudson* published to favourable reviews.

1876 Meets noted writers – Daudet, Flaubert, Zola, Turgenev, and others. In December, moves to London, taking rooms in Bolton Street, Piccadilly.

1877 Revisits France and Italy, publishes *The American*.

1878 *Watch and Ward* published as a book. Also publication of *The Europeans, Daisy Miller*, and first collection of criticism, *French Poets and Novelists*.

1879–80 Busy social life in London, further trips to the Continent. Works mainly on shorter fiction.

1881 Publishes *Washington Square* and *The Portrait of a Lady*, the latter mostly written during a long stay in Venice. Visits America late in the year.

1882 Mother dies in January while Henry is en route to Boston from Washington. He works on dramatization of *Daisy Miller,* returns to England in May, is called back to America in December upon fatal illness of his father.

1883 Returns to England. Death of Turgenev and of Garth Wilkinson James.

1884 Revisits Paris. Sister Alice arrives in England in November, a rather demanding invalid.

1885 Moves Alice to Bournemouth, where the ailing Robert Louis Stevenson is also staying; an earlier acquaintance between the two writers develops into friendship.

1886 James moves to 34 De Vere Gardens, Kensington. Publication of two novels, *The Bostonians* and *The Princess Casamassima,* both unappreciated at the time.

1887 Extended sojourn in Italy, chiefly in Florence and Venice.

1888 Brings out *The Reverberator,* 'The Aspern Papers', and works on *The Tragic Muse.* Travels in France, Switzerland, and Italy.

1889 Publishes a volume of tales, *A London Life.*

1890 Travels in Italy, publishes his novel of theatrical life, *The Tragic Muse.*

1891 The actor-producer Edward Compton stages James's dramatization of *The American,* played both on tour and in London, with moderate success.

1892 Publishes a volume of tales, *The Lesson of the Master.* Travels in Italy, writes the play *Disengaged.* Death of Alice James.

1893 Publishes two volumes of stories and two volumes of essays. Writes *Guy Domville,* a play.

1894 Writes the comedy, *Tenants,* which is not taken up by producers.

1895 *Guy Domville* produced in London – a fiasco. James publishes texts of two unproduced comedies and a volume of tales.

1896 Publication of the novel, *The Other House,* and a volume of stories, *Embarrassments.*

1897 Publication of *The Spoils of Poynton* and *What Maisie Knew.*

1898 Moves from London to Lamb House, Rye, Sussex.

1899 Spends Summer in Italy, publishes *The Awkward Age.*

1900 *The Soft Side,* a collection of stories.

1901 *The Sacred Fount,* a novel.

1902 Publication of *The Wings of the Dove,* the first of the great novels of his 'major phase' to appear.

1903 *The Ambassadors* published, also a two-volume biography *William Wetmore Story and His Friends,* dealing with an American painter in Rome.

1904 *The Golden Bowl,* the last of the three novels of the 'major phase'. Visits the United States for the first time since 1883.

1905 Travels in America, visiting Florida, the Middle West, and California, lecturing chiefly on

Balzac. Returns to Lamb House in summer.

1906–7 Works on revisions and Prefaces for the 'New York Edition' of *The Novels and Tales of Henry James.* Publishes *The American Scene.*

1908 Production of play, *The High Bid,* starring Johnston Forbes-Robertson, in Edinburgh and London, a mild success.

1909 A travel book, *Italian Hours.* Nervous illness in winter.

1910 Visits German spa with his ailing brother William, then returns with him to New Hampshire. Death of Robertson James in June, of William James in August.

1911 James remains in America until late July, is given an honorary degree by Harvard. After return to England begins work on autobiographical volumes.

1912 Takes London apartment, 21 Carlyle Mansions. Receives Honorary D.Litt. from Oxford.

1913 Seventieth birthday celebration, portrait by Sargent. Publication of *A Small Boy and Others.*

1914 Assists Allied War effort by visiting hospitals and writing essays. Second volume of autobiography published.

1915 Naturalized as British subject, 28 July. In December suffers stroke, followed by pneumonia.

1916 Awarded the Order of Merit by King George V on New Year's Day. Dies on 28 February.

BIBLIOGRAPHY

SOME BOOKS ABOUT HENRY JAMES

Everyone writing about Henry James, his life and his works, is profoundly indebted to Leon Edel, not only for his editing of many James texts and his accompanying critical comments, but also for his masterful five-volume biography, *The Life of Henry James* (1953–72), which is the single source for a great deal of knowledge about James; the present volume is greatly indebted to it for the essential lines of this account as well as for certain facts and anecdotes.

Some of the other books devoted to this author are:

Quentin Anderson: *The American Henry James* (1957)

Osborn Andreas: *Henry James and the Expanding Horizon* (1948)

Joseph Warren Beach: *The Method of Henry James* (1918)

Van Wyck Brooks: *The Pilgrimage of Henry James* (1925)

Oscar Cargill: *The Novels of Henry James* (1961)

Elizabeth Luther Cary: *The Novels of Henry James* (1906)

Seymour Chatman: *The Later Style of Henry James* (1972)

F. W. Dupee: *Henry James* (1951)
ed.: *The Question of Henry James* (1945)

Pelham Edgar: *Henry James: Man and Author* (1927)

Michael Egan: *Henry James: The Ibsen Years* (1972)

C. Hartley Grattan: *The Three Jameses* (1932)

D. W. Jefferson: *Henry James* (1960)

Cornelia Pulsifer Kelly: *The Early Development of Henry James* (1930)

James Kraft: *The Early Tales of Henry James* (1969)

Dorothea Krook: *The Ordeal of Consciousness in Henry James* (1962)

Robert Charles Le Clair: *The Young Henry James* (1955)

Robert Marks: *James's Later Novels* (1960)

H. O. Matthiessen: *Henry James: The Major Phase* (1944)
The James Family (1947)

Simon Noel-Smith, ed.: *The Legend of the Master* (1948)

Richard Poirier: *The Comic Sense of Henry James* (1960)

Lyall H. Powers: *Henry James: An Introduction and Interpretation* (1970)

S. Gorley Putt: *A Reader's Guide to Henry James* (1966)

Charles Thomas Samuels: *The Ambiguity of Henry James* (1966)

Elizabeth Stevenson: *The Crooked Corridor: A Study of Henry James* (1949)

Edward Stone: *The Battle of the Books: Some Aspects of Henry James* (1964)

Michael Swan: *Henry James* (1952)

Joseph A. Ward: *The Search for Form: Studies in the Structure of Henry James's Fiction* (1967)

Cristof Wegelin: *The Image of Europe in Henry James* (1958)

Philip M. Weinstein: *Henry James and the Requirements of the Imagination* (1972)

Muriel West: *A Stormy Night with 'The Turn of the Screw'* (1964)

Rebecca West: *Henry James* (1916)

Walter J. Wright: *The Madness of Art* (1962)

There are also many essays on Henry James in magazines and books. Some of the latter include:

Marius Bewley, *The Eccentric Design: Form in the Classic American Novel* (1959); R. P. Blackmur, *The Lion and the Honeycomb: Essays in Solicitude and Critique* (1955); Wayne C. Booth, *The Rhetoric of Fiction* (1961); Frederick J. Hoffman, *The Modern Novel in America* (1951); F. R. Leavis, *The Great Tradition: George Eliot, Henry James, Joseph Conrad* (1949); Harry T. Moore, *Age of the Modern* (1971); Wright Morris, *The Territory Ahead* (1958); Ezra Pound, *Make It New* (1935); Stephen Spender, *The Destructive Element* (1935); Tony Tanner, *The Reign of Wonder: Naivity and Reality in American Literature* (1965); Dorothy Van Ghent, *The English Novel: Form and Function* (1953); Austin Warren, *The New England Conscience* (1967); René Wellek, *A History of Modern Criticism: 1750–1950*, vol. IV (1965); Yvor Winters, *In Defense of Reason* (1947); Virginia Woolf, *The Death of the Moth and Other Essays* (1942); Morton Dauwen Zabel, *Craft and Character in Modern Fiction* (1957).

In 1913 Henry James drew up two reading lists of his work for a young man with literary ambitions (Stark Young) who had indirectly asked what he should read of James. These lists follow with the publication date of each novel added.

1. *Roderick Hudson* (1875), 2. *The Portrait of a Lady* (1881), 3. *The Princess Casamassima* (1886), 4. *The Wings of the Dove* (1902), 5. *The Golden Bowl* (1904).

James noted that the second list was, 'as it were, the more "advanced"'. It contained: 1. *The American* (1877), 2. *The Tragic Muse* (1889), 3. *The Wings of the Dove* (1902), 4. *The Ambassadors* (1903), 5. *The Golden Bowl* (1904). To the James enthusiast, all the novels are important, but readers who wish to follow this author from comparative simplicity to enriching complexity might also try *The Europeans* (1878), *Washington Square* (1881), *The Bostonians* (1886), *What Maisie Knew* (1897), and *The Sacred Fount* (1901). These novels may lead to still others.

As James commented when he made up the two lists of his novels, 'When it comes to the shorter Tales the question is more difficult [for characteristic selection] and requires separate treatment' – something he didn't undertake. Fortunately, however, Leon Edel has put *The Complete Tales of Henry James*, 112 of them, into twelve volumes (1961–64),

and even the earlier stories are of interest to readers beyond those concerned chiefly with James's development, for even that beginning work has its rewards. Some of the tales and novellas have been discussed in the present volume, among them the short novel *Daisy Miller* (1878), the most popular of all of James's works during his lifetime and still a first-rate story. Some of the others which readers may find particularly interesting are 'Madame de Mauves' (1874), 'Four Meetings' (1877), 'An International Episode' (1878), 'Lady Barberina' (1884), 'The Author of "Beltraffio"' (1884), 'The Aspern Papers' (1888), 'The Lesson of the Master' (1888) 'The Pupil' (1891), 'Owen Wingrave' (1892), 'The Death of the Lion' (1894), 'The Coxon Fund' (1894), 'The Figure in the Carpet' (1896), 'The Turn of the Screw' (1898), 'In the Cage' (1898), 'The Great Good Place' (1900), 'The Beast in the Jungle' (1903), 'The Jolly Corner' (1908), and 'The Bench of Desolation' (1909). These are a few of the most notable *Tales*, which can be found in Dr Edel's volumes or in other collections.

Henry James's three autobiographical books, *A Small Boy and Others* (1913), *Notes of a Son and Brother* (1914), and *The Middle Years* (1917; unfinished), have been brought together in a single volume, *Henry James: Autobiography* (1956), edited by F. W. Dupee. Percy Lubbock edited *The Letters of Henry James* (1920; 2 vols), and various other collections have appeared, including *Selected Letters of Henry James* (1955),

edited by Leon Edel who is preparing a larger edition of this material than has yet been published. James frequently wrote travel sketches describing various parts of Europe, as well as presenting his later-day impressions of his homeland in *The American Scene* (1907). Many of his best essays appeared in *The Art of Travel* (1958), edited by Morton Dauwen Zabel.

A continual observer of the literature of his time, James wrote extensive criticism collected in such volumes as *French Poets and Novelists* (1878), *Hawthorne* (1879; in the English Men of Letters series), *Views and Reviews* (1908; assembled by Le Roy Phillips), and *Notes on Novelists* (1914). R.P. Blackmur gathered together the notable prefaces James wrote for the 'New York Edition' of his fiction in *The Art of the Novel* (1934). F.O. Matthiessen and Kenneth B. Murdock made a valuable addition to James literature with their editing of *The Notebooks of Henry James* (1947). Leon Edel has brought out two further collections of James criticism in *The Future of the Novel* (1956) and *The House of Fiction* (1957).

Professor Edel has also edited *The Complete Plays of Henry James* (1949), whose introductory essay, 'Henry James: The Dramatic Years', provides a full and valuable account of that author's experiences in the theatre. Further, Dr. Edel has in association with Dan H. Laurence prepared *A Bibliography of Henry James* (1957), the fullest treatment of this aspect of Henry James.

LIST OF ILLUSTRATIONS

23 View of the Hospice of St Bernard; aquatint by J.-R. Bühlmann, *c.* 1860. Bibliothèque Publique et Universitaire, Geneva.

24 William James; photograph taken at the age of twenty-five. Houghton Library, reproduced by permission of the Harvard College Library.

Minny Temple; photograph taken at the age of sixteen.

25 *Prisoners from the Front*; oil-painting by Winslow Homer, 1866. The Metropolitan Museum of Art, Gift of Mrs Frank B. Porter, 1922.

Garth Wilkinson James in bed convalescing after Civil War wounds; drawing by William James, 1863. Houghton Library, reproduced by permission of the Harvard College Library.

26 The James family home 1860–62; Kay Street, Newport. Photo by courtesy of the author.

Dining-room at Hyanuary; engraving from Louis Agassiz, *A Journey in Brazil*, 1863.

27 Harvard Square; photograph taken in 1862. Boston Athenaeum. Photo courtesy Cambridge Historical Commission.

28 The James family home 1862–63; corner of Spring Street and Lee Avenue, Newport. Photo by courtesy of the author.

29 Charles Eliot Norton; photograph *c.* 1854 from *Letters of Charles Eliot Norton*, 1913.

Henry James; oil-painting by John La Farge, *c.* 1860. Collection Century Association. Photo courtesy Frick Art Reference Library, New York.

James Russell Lowell; photograph *c.* 1865 from *Letters of Charles Eliot Norton*, 1913.

30 Morley's Hotel, Trafalgar Square; photograph *c.* 1880. Radio Times Hulton Picture Library.

31 Henry James Sr; photograph taken in middle life. Houghton Library, reproduced by permission of the Harvard College Library.

View near Tewkesbury; drawing from Henry James's sketchbook, 1869.

32 William Morris; portrait attributed to Charles Fairfax-Murray, *c.* 1870. National Portrait Gallery, London.

George Eliot; drawing by Sir W. F. Burton, 1865. National Portrait Gallery, London.

33 Dante Gabriel Rossetti; photograph by Lewis Carroll, 1863. Gernsheim Collection, University of Texas.

John Ruskin; portrait by John Everett Millais, 1853–54. Collection Mrs Patrick Gibson.

34 Robertson James; photograph, 1891. Houghton Library, reproduced by permission of the Harvard College Library.

35 Henry James; sketch by William James, *c.* 1873. Houghton Library, reproduced by permission of the Harvard College Library.

Alice James; sketch by Henry James from a letter, 23 May 1872. Houghton Library, reproduced by permission of the Harvard College Library.

36 John Hay (1838–1905); portrait by John Singer Sargent. Courtesy John Hay.

Emile Zola; portrait by Edouard Manet, 1868. Louvre, Paris. Photo Bulloz.

37 Gustave Flaubert (1821–80); photograph by Nadar. Archives Photographiques.

Ivan Turgenev (1818–83); photograph by Nadar. Archives Photographiques.

38 *Mr James in London*; by Max Beerbohm from his *Book of Caricatures*, 1907.

Frontispiece to 'In the Cage'; photograph by Alvin Langdon Coburn for the 'New York Edition' of Henry James's *Collected Novels*, 1908.

39 Cover of the pirate edition of *The American*, London, 1877.

40 First page of the autograph manuscript of *The Europeans*. Photo courtesy Sotheby's, London.

41 Henry James; caricature by Max Beerbohm, probably related to James's essay on D'Annunzio published in 1904: '. . . it has no more dignity . . . than the boots and shoes we see, in the corridors of promiscuous hotels, standing, often in double pairs, at the doors of rooms.' Ashmolean Museum, Oxford.

42 *Afternoon, Pincian Hill*; watercolour by Maurice Prendergast, 1898. The Phillips Collection, Washington.

43 'Marion Almond came up to Catherine in company with a tall young man'; illustration to *Washington Square* from *Cornhill Magazine*, 1880.

44 William James, self-portrait sketch, 1866. Houghton Library, reproduced by permission of the Harvard College Library.

45 4161 Riva degli Schiavoni, Venice, where James took a room in 1881. Photo by courtesy of the author.

46–47 Piazzetta di San Marco; late 19th-century photograph. Radio Times Hulton Picture Library.

48 Elizabeth Boott Duveneck and her father, Francis Boott, with Frank Duveneck and Mrs Duveneck's nurse, Mary Ann Shenstone; photograph taken at the Villa Castellani, Bellosguardo, c. 1890. Photo by courtesy of the author.

50 Mrs Henry James Sr; photograph c. 1880.

51 Henry James in 1882; wood engraving by Timothy Cole for the November issue of *Century Magazine*.

'Boston Aestheticism versus Oscar Wilde. The Old Lady of Beacon Hill: "No sir, shoddy New York may receive you with open arms, but we have an Aestheticism of our own."' *Daily Graphic*, New York, 19 January 1882.

52 *Boston Common at Twilight*; oil-painting by Childe Hassam, 1885–86. Courtesy Museum of Fine Arts, Boston. Gift of Miss Maud E. Appleton.

53 Henry James Sr; portrait by Frank Duveneck, c. 1880. Houghton Library, reproduced by permission of the Harvard College Library.

54 John Singer Sargent; caricature by Max Beerbohm, c. 1900. Tate Gallery, London.

54–55 View of the beach at Bournemouth; photograph c. 1880. Radio Times Hulton Picture Library.

55 Robert Louis Stevenson; portrait by John Singer Sargent, 1884. The Taft Museum, Cincinnati.

56 Alice James and Katherine Loring in Leamington; photograph taken in the early 1880s. Houghton Library, reproduced by permission of the Harvard College Library.

57 Alice James; photograph taken by Katherine Loring. Houghton Library, reproduced by permission of the Harvard College Library.

58 34 De Vere Gardens, Kensington, where James lived 1886–96. Photo from *The Complete Plays of Henry James*.

60 *Interior of a Palazzo in Venice*; oil-painting by John Singer Sargent, 1899. Burlington House, London. Photo Royal Academy of Arts.

61 The Rialto Bridge and the Grand Canal; late 19th century photograph. Radio Times Hulton Picture Library.

62 Constance Fenimore Woolson; photograph c. 1885.

'Juliana's Court'; frontispiece by Alvin Langdon Coburn to 'The Aspern Papers' for the New York Edition of Henry James's *Collected Novels*, 1908.

63 Palazzo Barbaro, Venice, where James stayed in 1887. Photo Alinari.

65 Edward Compton as Christopher Newman in *The American* at the Opera Comique, London, 1891. Raymond Mander and Joe Mitchenson Theatre Collection.

Programme of *The American*, 1891. Raymond Mander and Joe Mitchenson Theatre Collection.

66 Elizabeth Robins in one of her non-Ibsen roles; photograph signed by her for James, 1874. Houghton Library, reproduced by permission of the Harvard College Library.

67 Caricature of Elizabeth Robins as Claire in *The American*; from *Illustrated Sporting and Dramatic News*, 1891. Photo by courtesy of the author.

68 James's list of possible titles for *Disengaged*. Photo from *The Complete Plays of Henry James*.

69 British Broadcasting Corporation's production of Benjamin Britten's opera *Owen Wingrave*, 1971. Photo BBC.

70 Back cover of volume 1 of *The Yellow Book*, April 1894. Courtesy Eve Garrett.

71 Letter from James to Edmund Gosse on the occasion of Robert Louis Stevenson's death, 17 December 1894. British Museum, London.

72 St James's Theatre, 1896. Raymond Mander and Joe Mitchenson Theatre Collection.

George Alexander as Guy Domville, 1894. Raymond Mander and Joe Mitchenson Theatre Collection.

73 Scene from *Guy Domville*, St James's Theatre, 1894; left to right: Herbert Waring as Frank Humber, Marion Terry as Mrs Peverel, George Alexander as Guy Domville and W.G. Eliot as Lord Deverish. Raymond Mander and

Joe Mitchenson Theatre Collection.

75 Gertrude Elliott as Mrs Gracedew in *The High Bid*, which had two performances at the After Noon Theatre at His Majesty's, 18 February 1909. Raymond Mander and Joe Mitchenson Theatre Collection.

Gertrude Elliott and Edmund Sass, as Mr Prodmore, in *The High Bid*, Act III. Photo from *The Complete Plays of Henry James*.

76 Henry James; portrait by Philip Burne-Jones, 1894. Lamb House, Rye.

77 Page from James's notebook, 14 February 1895. Photo by courtesy of the author.

78– The harbour, Torquay; late 19th-
79 century photograph. Radio Times Hulton Picture Library.

80 Henry James on the steps of the Palazzo Borghese, Rome, 1890. Photo by Count Giuseppe Primoli. Houghton Library, reproduced by permission of the Harvard College Library.

81 View of the studio, Lamb House, Rye. Photo by courtesy of the author.

Façade of Lamb House, Rye. Photo British Tourist Authority.

82 Illustration to *The Turn of the Screw* by Philippe Jullian, 1946. Courtesy Tambimuttu at the Lyrebird Press.

Henry James, 1897; drawing by William Rothenstein, 1897. Lamb House, Rye.

84 Henry James; photograph *c.* 1900. Photo by courtesy of the author.

85 Violet Hunt; photograph from her autobiography *The Flurried Years*, 1926.

A memory of Henry James and Joseph Conrad conversing at an afternoon party, circa 1904; caricature by Max Beerbohm, 1926. Humanities Research Center, University of Texas at Austin, Austin, Texas.

86 Autographed programme of *The Ghost*, performed at Brede School House, 1899. Columbia University Library.

87 Henry James with Cora Crane at a garden fête at Brede Rectory; photograph 1899. Columbia University Library.

Henry James with Edith and Teddy Wharton in her Panhard, 1907. Photo courtesy Leon Edel and Granada Publishing Limited.

88 Illustration to 'The Beast in the Jungle', by Charles Demuth, *c.* 1924. Photo Peter A. Juley, New York.

89 W. D. Howells; photograph by Alvin Langdon Coburn from *Men of Mark*, 1913.

90 Place de l'Opéra; painting by Jean Béraud, 1901. Private Collection. Photo courtesy Ferrers Gallery, London.

91 Luxembourg Gardens, *c.* 1900. Photo Collection Georges Sirot.

92 'A Henry James sentence'; cartoon published in the United States during his visit in 1905–6. From a scrapbook in the New York Public Library.

93 Portrait of Lucrezia Panciatichi by Agnólo Bronzino (1503–72). Uf-

fizi, Florence. Photo Mansell-Alinari.

94 Henry James in the garden of Lamb House, 1901. Lamb House, Rye.

95 Henry James and Mrs Humphry Ward in the garden at Lamb House. Lamb House, Rye.

96 Theodora Bosanquet; photograph at Lamb House, Rye.

Burgess Noakes; photograph at Lamb House, Rye.

97 Interior of the Athenaeum Club. Radio Times Hulton Picture Library.

Reform Club; engraving 1893. Radio Times Hulton Picture Library.

98 *Mr Henry James revisiting America*; by Max Beerbohm from *A Book of Caricatures*, 1907.

99 95 Irving Street, Cambridge, Massachusetts; William James's house. Photo courtesy of John S. R. James.

101 Henry and William James; photograph taken during Henry's American visit, 1905. Lamb House, Rye.

Henry James in New York in the studio of Alice Broughton, 1906. Photo by courtesy of the author.

102 Henry James on the terrace at Vallombrosa with Howard Sturgis and the Boits, 1907. Houghton Library, reproduced by permission of the Harvard College Library.

Hendrik Andersen's bust of Henry James in his studio in Rome. Photo by courtesy of the author.

103 Hendrik Andersen's sculptures in his studio in Rome. Photo by courtesy of the author.

104 Hugh Walpole as a young man. Photo by courtesy of the author.

105 H. G. Wells; photograph *c.* 1904. Radio Times Hulton Picture Library.

107 Opening of *Oedipus the King*, Covent Garden, 1912. Raymond Mander and Joe Mitchenson Theatre Collection.

109 Leslie Howard as Peter Standish in a scene from the second production of *Berkeley Square* at the Lyric Theatre, London, 1928. Raymond Mander and Joe Mitchenson Theatre Collection.

110 Henry James; portrait by John Singer Sargent, 1913. National Portrait Gallery, London.

112 Carlyle Mansions, Chelsea. Photo Andrew Lee.

View of Rye. Radio Times Hulton Picture Library.

113 Edmund Gosse; portrait by John Singer Sargent. National Portrait Gallery, London.

Letter from James to Edmund Gosse, July 1915. Lamb House, Rye.

114 Winston Churchill addressing workers at a meeting in Enfield, 1915. Radio Times Hulton Picture Library.

115 Grande Place, Ypres, 1916. Imperial War Museum, London.

116 Memorial plaque in Chelsea Old Church. By courtesy of the Vicar of Chelsea Old Church. Photo Andrew Lee.

INDEX